FLORAL
ART
IN THE
CHURCH

FLORAL ART IN THE CHURCH

JACK INMAN

PHOTOGRAPHS BY RICHARD T. LEE

Abingdon Press
NASHVILLE
NEW YORK

SET UP, PRINTED, AND BOUND BY THE
PARTHENON PRESS, AT NASHVILLE,
TENNESSEE, UNITED STATES OF AMERICA

dedicated to
the fellowship of
Belle Meade Methodist Church
who first gave me
the privilege of preparing
the altar flowers

CONTENTS

INTRODUCTION

Flowers have been used in religious ceremonies throughout recorded history and appear to have been important as decorations and offerings in virtually all religions. Egyptian stone carvings made as early as 2500 B.C. show floral arrangements made for this purpose. We know that the Mayans, Greeks, and Romans not only used flowers in worship, but emphasized their symbolic meanings. Flowers have been used in holy places in India and China for untold centuries, and since the introduction of Buddhism to Japan in the sixth century, the Japanese have placed flowers in Buddhist monasteries and before images of Buddha. Indeed, flowers are used in the religious rites of many primitive cultures.

Thus the floral offering is not only a Christian tradition, but tends to be a part of the religious observances of all mankind. The fact that flowers or evergreens are readily available in most of the world and that they present a lovely appearance but are relatively inexpensive has undoubtedly played a part in this tradition. In arranging flowers to use in his places of worship, man seems to find a convenient way to offer his gods something of beauty and at the same time to find aesthetic satisfaction himself.

In thinking of flower arranging as we are concerned with it here, we must consider it as liturgical art—an art form which is an aid to worship. The floral offering will come under this category if it is well conceived and properly constructed, taking into consideration the service for which it will be used and the church in which it is to go. Too often art in churches, and for us specifically the flower arrangement, is used purely as decoration. Properly, liturgical art should strive to communicate and interpret and to increase our awareness of the divine. When art is used to underline the meaning of the service as an aid in worship, it becomes sacred.

"Architecture will dictate the decoration" is a well-known aphorism and one much used by floral designers. There can hardly be much argument with this statement, but it should be a starting point for the creative designer. The arrangement must agree in tone with its surroundings, but it must also express the season and the service for which it is used. To arrange flowers to be suitable for a given church, one should be familiar with its particular style, know how the various areas are intended to be used, and be aware of the symbolic background of each area. Regardless of the architecture of your church, you should find real challenge and reward in achieving suitable floral designs for it.

Floral arrangement, like other creative art forms, reflects the life and styles of the times. Today we lean toward simplicity of line and design in our arrangements; we have discarded the vogue for great masses of flowers in favor of fewer, better arranged specimens which express more forcefully the intended symbolism. When little or no emphasis has been given in your church to the symbolism of the altar flowers, an explanation and interpretation might be placed in the church bulletin to help develop understanding and appreciation for this form of expression.

Several basic shapes in floral design are also basic Christian symbols. These may be utilized with appropriate flowers to express symbolically the message or observance of the day. The equilateral triangle is the symbol of the Trinity, placing equal emphasis on belief in the Father, Son, and Holy Spirit. The circle represents the everlasting and continuing love of God. It may also express the all-inclusiveness of the Christian church and the brotherhood of all men. The crescent has for many centuries been the symbol for Mary, the mother of Jesus. The torch symbolizes the search for knowledge. This vertical design is often used to express the zeal and urgency with which the message of God is carried forth, or it may represent man's upward reach for God.

Traditionally, living flowers are placed on the altar of the church to celebrate Christ's victory over death. For this reason many churches will not permit artificial flowers or greens within the chancel. The decorative wrappings and ribbons with which potted plants are often decorated may detract from the beauty of the plants and are out of character with the appointments of the chancel. Your florist will be happy to deliver plants with plain plastic covers of soft brown and green.

If your flowers are purchased regularly, you should find a good florist who will be conscious of your needs and willing to secure special requirements. The best source of supply may be from the gardens of church members, the church garden, or plantings on church property. Let the people responsible for the floral offering know of the sources and the budget allowance when this is needed. Provide them with supplies at the church including floral foam (oasis), tape, wire, tools, needle holders, and anchoring material.

Planning is important! The minister will provide the schedule of services and other information which you will need. The following suggested planning sheet is included for guidance in developing a system adapted to and suitable for your own local church schedule and worship. The sample sheet includes the day, the assignment, the liturgical color, the theme or observance, the selection of candles, the type and symbolism of the floral offerings, and a record of memorial gifts. It indicates that the planning began with a season, and this may be

practical if your church follows the Christian year. No less than one month—
and perhaps three—is a good period of time to consider, but experience
will determine how far in advance this planning must be done and
how soon assignments are to be given.

It is hoped that the illustrations in this book will be helpful in your planning.
They represent flowers suitable for all types of Protestant churches—from
the small rural chapel to the large church in the city. Even the smallest church
can present a lovely floral offering, for it is not the size of the arrangement
that matters but the symbolic expression carried by well-chosen and
thoughtfully handled materials. We have a rich heritage of Christian
symbolism, and here we have the opportunity to express it in the use
of plants and flowers. This book has been written in the
hope of encouraging such expression.

PLANNING SHEET

Advent and Christmastide

DATE	ASSIGNMENT	COLOR	THEME	CANDLES	SYMBOLS & FLOWERS	MEMORIAL
11/29	Smith	Violet	Preparation	One purple	Advent wreath Roses—messianic promise Pine branches—Jesse tree	Clark
12/6	Ross	Violet	Penitence Communion	Two purple	Chalice—the cup Grapes—fruit of the vine	
12/13	Mason	Violet	Humility	Three purple	The Bible—word & spirit	Levinson
12/20	Lovell & Black	Violet	Love	Four purple	Rose—love	Gibson
12/24	Committee	Violet	Communion	Four purple and one white Candelabra	Green trees, poinsettias	Wright
12/25	Garvin	White	Gloria	Same	Same	
12/27	Russel!	White	Mary	Two white	Holly crescent One white flower	

Note: Order poinsettia plants for chancel and narthex by December 1.
Advise Communion steward of the two services in December.
Get copy for the memorial flowers to the church office on Wednesday.

THE CHRISTIAN YEAR

The Christian calendar is divided into seasons instead of days and months. This seasonal chronology has been observed since the early centuries of the Christian era. Most Protestant denominations have adopted this pattern to some extent, at least, in appreciation of its value as a means of emphasizing the great truths of the faith. It is helpful as an orderly guide for teaching and worship and ensures the witness of the "whole gospel."

The year is divided into halves. The first half, from Advent through Eastertide, deals with God's revelation to man through the life and the ministry of Jesus. The second half, from Pentecost through Kingdomtide, has to do with man's commitment, or response, to this revelation—a time for Christian instruction and growth in discipleship.

There is no liturgical guide for the use of flowers during the Christian year. Seasonal symbolism, liturgical colors, and, above all, good taste chiefly determine the choice of plants and flowers.

Through careful attention to detail in arrangement flowers can be made to serve as vivid symbols of age-old religious truths when used in altar arrangements.

For the observance of the Christian year by your church, consult your minister and the ritual or manual of worship to determine the choice of seasons and special days. This book deals with the year as generally adopted by Protestant churches but will perhaps not follow exactly the pattern of every denomination—it is, in fact, merely the record of what one church did with its altar arrangements.

ADVENT

The Season

Advent is considered the beginning of the Christian year. It starts on the Sunday *nearest* November 30 and lasts until Christmas Day, a period which includes four Sundays. The name comes from the Latin *advenire*, meaning "to come to," for Advent is the time of preparation for the Saviour's coming into the world.

The season is a time of promise and hope, of prayer and expectancy, of self-examination and self-denial. It developed out of the early Christian practice of having candidates for membership observe a fasting period prior to their reception into the church on Epiphany. With the acceptance of the Christmas festival this period of preparation gradually became a custom observed by the Christian community.

Violet (purple in some churches) is the color generally used for Advent. It is symbolic of penitence, watching, and fasting, as Christians prepare themselves to be ready for the Feast of the Nativity, or Christmas, the glorious celebration of the birth of Jesus.

PREPARATION AND PROPHECY

First Sunday in Advent

Symbolism

Isaiah's Prophecy of Jesus' Lineage: Jesse Tree

Messianic Promise: Rose

Eternal Love and Existence of God: Circle, Evergreen Wreath

The Light Christ Brings into the World: Candle

During Advent, on each of the four Sundays preceding Christmas, the thought of the church is directed toward the coming of the Christ Child. Isaiah prophesied long before Jesus was born that "there shall come forth a rod out of the stem of Jesse, and a Branch shall grow out of his roots" (Isaiah 11:1). At the coming of this Messiah all things would be made new, Isaiah said. "The desert shall rejoice and blossom as the rose" at the coming of the glory of God (Isa. 35:1). Christians applied these prophecies to the birth of Jesus, and through the ages the Jesse tree and the blooming rose have reminded us of Christ's fulfilling of the Old Testament prophecy.

The evergreen, a symbol of eternal life in ages previous to the Christian era, was adopted by the Christian church early in its history. In the form of a circle, another ancient symbol of endless time, it is used to remind Christians of the everlasting love of God.

Christians use candles throughout the liturgical year, but during Advent their light takes on a special meaning. It reminds us of the light Christ brings into the world.

The Altar: In the arrangement shown, the traditional Advent wreath is being used. A single candle indicates that this is the first Sunday in Advent. Violet, the color of the season, is used for the candle as well as for the paraments. A simple design of roses and evergreen branches suggests the Old Testament prophecies that Christ came to fulfill.

Suggestions: A wreath can be made from pine, balsam, spruce, cedar, or any other handy evergreen. If sprinkled occasionally and refrigerated between Sundays, one wreath can be made to last the entire season.

PENITENCE
Second Sunday in Advent*

Symbolism

Eternal Love of God: Circle, Advent Wreath

Holy Communion: Chalice

Consecrated Wine: Grapes

Human and Divine Natures of Christ: Two Candles

Messianic Promise: Poinsettias

The experience of Communion during Advent adds to the seasonal emphasis on penitence. A chalice filled with grapes may represent the cup and the wine which are consecrated for the sacrament. Two candles at Communion always symbolize the human and divine natures of Jesus, and this Sunday they also represent the second Sunday in Advent.

The Altar: On this Communion Sunday work out the best arrangement with your minister. Since the Communion elements are on the altar table, hang a wreath of berried holly above the altar. Place a chalice in front of the wreath and use red poinsettias and red candles on each side.

Red or white poinsettias may be used in other areas of the chancel or nave. Order your plants early and specify delivery with green or brown plastic pot covers so they will not arrive with the usual decorative ribbon and paper wrappings.

Suggestions: If the Advent wreath is left on the altar table and the Communion is served from another table, place a chalice-type container filled with fresh purple grapes in the center of the wreath. If the two candles are a part of the wreath, the setting may seem too crowded, in which case it may be possible to elevate the chalice of grapes on a shelf behind the altar table, or it might even be best to elevate both grapes and candles.

*Many churches observe Universal Bible Sunday on either the second or third Sunday in Advent. See the section on special observances for this.

HUMILITY
Third Sunday in Advent

Symbolism
Humility: Fern
Messianic Promise: White Poinsettias
Eternal Love of God: Circle, Advent Wreath
The Passing of the Advent Season: Three Candles

This Sunday the floral offering stresses the humility which one should feel as the celebration of the Nativity draws near. By lighting three candles we are reminded that the Advent season is passing. The fern speaks of humility, and the white poinsettias stand for the messianic promise; the combination is symbolic of humble expectation, which we experience as did the prophets.

The Altar: Side arrangements of large fern foliage with poinsettia flowers are effective today. If the wreath you have been using is showing signs of drying, you might make a fresh one of soft ferns and scatter small white poinsettias through it. If your original wreath is still in good condition, you can simply add the poinsettias to it. Three candles are used with the wreath.

Suggestions: If you use poinsettia plants for this altar arrangement instead of just the blossoms, you can keep them fresh by enclosing the roots and soil in plastic bags. The roots can then be concealed in the arrangement. Potted poinsettias and fern plants may be used.

LOVE
Fourth Sunday in Advent

Advent
Fourth Sunday
Color: Violet

Symbolism
Eternal Love of God: Circle, Advent Wreath
Pure Love of God: White Rose
Messianic Promise: White Poinsettia
Eternal Love: Green Trees
The Passing of the Advent Season: Four Candles

"For God so loved the world, that he gave his only begotten Son."
These familiar words provide the theme for our design today. The eternal
love of God is expressed by the use of the Advent wreath, and the purity
of his love is spoken of by the white roses in its center.

The Altar: Four lighted candles are set at regular intervals around the Advent
wreath, and a slender arrangement of white rosebuds is placed inside the
wreath. Evergreen trees, live and unadorned, may be grouped near the altar
on either side with white poinsettias banked at the base of the trees.

Suggestions: If you prefer to have the candles set within the wreath, the roses
could be placed to either side of it. If the Advent wreath is not used,
the trees and poinsettias are still quite effective alone.

GLORY TO GOD
Christmas Eve Communion

Symbolism

Glory of God: Laurel Branches

Eternal Love of God: Circle, Advent Wreath

Four Sundays in Advent: Four Purple Candles

Jesus—the Light of the World: One Large White Candle

This Communion is the final service in preparation for the celebration of Christmas; in fact, many churches hold the service at 11:00 P.M. so that the last portion of it actually falls on Christmas Day. The lighting, the flowers, and the music are all planned to emphasize the deep joy and solemn beauty of this holy night.

The Altar: A large white candle is set in the center of the altar and encircled by the Advent wreath. The four purple Advent candles are spaced at even intervals within the wreath. Laurel may be used for accent in the wreath. Carefully placed groupings of evergreen trees, laurel branches, and white poinsettias are appropriate for use in the chancel.

Suggestions: Laurel branches, because they symbolize triumph and glory, are especially suitable to this service; but since they will not be available in all parts of the country at this time, you may substitute other evergreen branches for a quite satisfactory effect.

The use of many candles throughout the chancel and nave adds to the beauty of this service.

CHRISTMASTIDE

The Season

Christmastide covers the twelve-day period from Christmas Day on December 25 to Epiphany on January 6. It usually includes two Sundays.

Christmas was not a festival held by the earliest church, and even after its acceptance there was controversy for a long time over the proper time for its observance. The argument was especially heated over whether it should be established on December 25 or January 6, although other dates were considered as well. The date was finally set in 440 and was chosen to coincide with that of the pagan feast of the winter solstice, which had its origins long before written history.

Most primitive peoples seem at some point of their development to have been sun worshipers. At the time of the solstice elaborate feasts were held in Egypt, Persia, and southern Europe, while in northern Europe great bonfires were lighted to give the winter sun god strength and to bring him back to life. When it became apparent that the days were in fact growing a few minutes longer, there was great feasting and rejoicing. The central idea in the celebration of the winter solstice—the return of light—became in the celebration of Christmas the coming of Jesus, the light of the world.

It would be possible to trace the origins of the many customs that we love today, but it is enough for our purposes to realize that the American celebration holds elements taken from the festival as celebrated in different parts of the world, and that it is based on rites dating back to prehistoric man as well as later customs developed by the church. The season is one of great joy, of fulfillment to mankind of the promise of the coming of a Messiah, and it is fitting that it should embody portions of festivals evolved over countless centuries.

The color for Christmastide is white, which signifies the Godhead, purity, light, and rejoicing.

CHRISTMAS DAY
The Birth of Christ

Symbolism
Pure Love: White Rose
Joy: Candles

Most churches are open on Christmas Day for all who wish to come for meditation and thanksgiving. A visit to the church on Christmas morning is traditional with many families.

The Altar: The additional candles used throughout the chancel for the Christmas Eve service are not needed today. Some of the greenery used to decorate the chancel could also be removed, and the greenery that remains should be fresh. A simple setting of candles, a few roses, and greenery provides the best background for quiet, personal meditations.

Suggestions: The altar candles will probably need to be replaced. They are ordinarily lighted before the church is officially opened and left burning until it is closed.

If your church has been using an Advent wreath, it is still appropriate today.

HONORING MARY
THE MOTHER OF JESUS
First Sunday After Christmas Day

Symbolism
Mary, Mother of Jesus: Crescent
Humility: Fern, Broom
Innocence: Daisy
Purity: White Orchid
The Holy Night: White Poinsettia

The first Sunday following Christmas is set aside to honor Mary, the Mother of Jesus. For centuries in Christian art and literature her symbol has been the crescent. Fern is used to express the humility with which the Virgin responded to the Annunciation, and the white flowers symbolize the innocence of the newborn Jesus as well as the purity of Mary's love for her child.

The Altar: The fern is arranged in a gentle crescent with white orchids or poinsettias featured at the central point of interest. Broom may be used in place of the fern and lends itself nicely to this type of arrangement.

Suggestion: If these materials aren't locally available, try holly with some other variety of large white flower.

PEACE ON EARTH
GOOD WILL TO MEN
Second Sunday After Christmas Day*

Symbolism
Good Will: Holly
Peace: Mistletoe, Verbena, Myrtle, Olive Branch
Love: Red Roses

"Glory to God in the highest, and on earth peace, good will toward men."
The Christmas hymn of praise first sung by the angel choir gives us our theme
for today as we reaffirm our delight and joy at the birth of Christ and renew
our commitment to bring peace and good will to all men.

The Altar: Burfordi, Chinese, or Foster holly in a horizontal arrangement
can be used to make an evergreen floral offering which is simple and
meaningful without the addition of flowers. If your chancel permits, you may
want to try a mass of roses centered at the altar with side arrangements of
green holly or one of the other types of greenery suggested above. A number
of white candles effectively placed help express the joy and happiness of this
day.

Suggestions: If you wish to make a more colorful arrangement, add red or
white rosebuds. This is especially good in a hogarth design.** Try twin hogarth
arrangements for an unusual and interesting effect.

---

*Some churches celebrate Student Sunday at this time. See the special observances section
for this service.
**The hogarth design, one of the most popular designs in American flower arrangement, is a
curving line known as Hogarth's "line of beauty."

COMMITMENT
New Year's Eve Watch Night Service

Symbolism
Devotion: Cornflower, Azalea
Faithfulness: Carnation
Reliability: Chrysanthemum
Strength: Bamboo, Cedar, Pine

This is a service in which Christians renew their commitment to God. It is an opportunity for rededication, a time to consecrate anew one's life to the service of Christ. The mood is one of simplicity and sincerity in keeping with the seriousness of the occasion.

The Altar: A simple arrangement of two, perhaps three, of the materials above will express the dominant theme of this service. A combination of bamboo and chrysanthemums lends itself readily to a simple, striking arrangement. Potted live azaleas are effective. Carnations combined with cedar are always good.

EPIPHANY

The Season

Epiphany starts on January 6 and runs until Ash Wednesday. There will be from four to nine Sundays in this season.

The name Epiphany is derived from a Greek word meaning "appearance" or "manifestation," and the date was at one time celebrated as both the birth and baptism of Jesus. In Protestant churches Epiphany has come to be celebrated primarily in commemoration of the coming of the Magi, who were Gentiles—not Jews—and were thus the first Gentiles to whom Christ was made manifest. From this comes one of the themes of Epiphany: the missionary work of the church.

With the exception of Easter, Epiphany is the oldest Christian festival. The star of Bethlehem is the symbol of the season,* and the flowers used during this period should be bright and rich in texture, symbolizing the royal gifts brought by the Wise Men who followed that star.

White is the color for Epiphany Day (January 6), and many churches use green thereafter. Some churches use white for the Sunday following Epiphany Day, designating this as Epiphany Sunday.

*Note that the star is appropriate to this season and not to Christmastide.

EPIPHANY DAY

Symbolism
Christ Manifested to the Gentiles: Star of Bethlehem
The Magi: Three Candles
The Three Gifts: Three Flowers

The coming of the three Wise Men to Bethlehem is significant as the first recognition that Jesus was not to be just King of the Jews, but a Saviour to all men. Today's design attempts to represent the Magi, while the gifts that they brought will be stressed separately on the next three Sundays.

The Altar: If the chancel arrangement permits it, hang a star of Bethlehem above and behind the altar. This star should be simple (not ornate or tinseled); one made of rattan in a dull gold finish would be good.

Make a simple design using three strelitzia (bird-of-paradise) with ti leaves added for support and accent. Three candles placed appropriately would add balance.

Suggestion: The strelitzia is chosen for its brilliant color and regal appearance. Zingiber (ginger) or any other beautiful flower of royal color and bearing may be substituted.

THE GIFT OF GOLD
First Sunday After Epiphany Day

Symbolism
Dignity: Chrysanthemum
Virtue, Worth, Divinity: Gold
The Three Gifts: Three Candles

Gold was one of the first metals known to man, probably because it is found in nature in an almost pure state and can be refined and worked with simple tools. It is mentioned hundreds of times in the Bible, usually with emphasis on it as a precious metal. Because it has historically been accepted as valuable and as a symbol of wealth, it is appropriate as one of the three gifts brought to the Christ Child.

In today's arrangement we stress the color gold and represent the winding route of the Magi by the use of twisted vines. Three candles remind us of the three gifts.

The Altar: A modern arrangement using three large chrysanthemums in either yellow or bronze in combination with vines or wisteria branches sprayed with gold, or in combination with driftwood, would be effective. Yellow-gold croton leaves make good accents. This design is very impressive if placed in a chest-type bronze (or wood painted to look like bronze) container. Three candles may be placed as seems best to you.

THE GIFT OF
FRANKINCENSE
Second Sunday After Epiphany Day

Symbolism
Purity: White Rose
The Three Gifts: Three Candles

In Jewish tradition frankincense was one of the ingredients in the incense burned before the Holy of Holies. This fragrant gum resin from Arabian trees emits a balsam-like odor while burning. Since the incense burned in the temple was used to purify the sanctuary, this gift symbolizes at once Jesus' inherent purity and his worthiness of the holy gift of frankincense. Christ, then, is acknowledged to have dominion over religious observances in this world and in the next.

The Altar: White roses are arranged with cedar and a few bits of baby's breath (gypsophila). An incense burner is used to represent the frankincense.

Suggestion: Lilies can be substituted for the roses, spruce or balsam for the cedar.

THE GIFT OF MYRRH
Third Sunday After Epiphany Day

Symbolism
Grief, Sorrow: Thorn, Cyclamen
Duty Through Hardships: Plum
Happiness: Orange Blossom
The Three Gifts: Three Candles

The third Wise Man brought myrrh, a reddish-brown, aromatic gum resin with a bitter, slightly pungent taste. The plant from which myrrh is obtained is a thorny shrub which bears small flowers and plumlike fruits. Myrrh was used in antiquity as an embalming substance and as an ingredient in the holy oil used for anointing. The gift of myrrh gives us a premonition of the bitter sorrows awaiting the Christ Child here on earth. It brings to mind Jesus' future suffering and his burial in the tomb. But this is not the end, for although myrrh symbolizes Christ's entombment, the gift also acknowledges Christ's final victory: the glorious dominion over death.

The Altar: A tall, slender pitcher with a gold or bronze finish makes a good container. A fine arrangement can be made of pyracantha, thorns, and plums or plum-colored chrysanthemums.

Suggestions: Myrrh branches are excellent if they are available. Crown of thorns would also do nicely. Orange blossoms and/or cyclamen can be used with the thorns. Twin arrangements with the candles centered in between would emphasize the dual symbolism of this gift: death and, at the same time, victory over death.

PRESENTATION OF JESUS IN THE TEMPLE
Fourth Sunday After Epiphany Day

Symbolism
Old Testament Worship: Menorah
New Testament Teachings: Torch
Innocence: Daisy
Purity: Camellia, Cherry Blossoms, Iris, Orchid, Gardenia, Lily of the Valley
Devotion: Daffodil, Cornflower, Narcissus, Hawthorn

Jesus' presentation in the temple was an important occasion in his life, for at that time old prophecies were fulfilled. The symbols we use today remind us that Christ is the link between Old Testament worship and New Testament promise. The menorah, or seven-branched candelabrum, brings to mind the early life of Jesus while the torch stands for the teachings he later gave to the world, as recorded in the New Testament.

The Altar: Place a menorah in the center of the altar table and use a torch design of pink daisies and heather on each side. Cherry branches with hawthorn or narcissus are good for this. Gardenias with their own foliage and lilies of the valley also make a pleasing combination, or you may wish to use some of the other flowers suggested above.

Suggestions: You may be able to borrow an authentic menorah from a Jewish friend, but if this is not possible, an ordinary seven-branched candelabrum should prove satisfactory.

An effective alternate arrangement utilizes a pair of candelabra with smaller torch arrangements on either side of the altar. These could be put on stands if the arrangement of the chancel requires it.

DEVOTION
Fifth Sunday After Epiphany Day

Symbolism

Devotion: Bamboo, Narcissus, Azalea, Daffodil

Every Christian should be devoted to the missionary efforts of his church. Today we point out our concern for this responsibility by emphasizing the message of the Epiphany season: the manifestation of Christ to the Gentiles. We try to express the devotion that this task requires.

The Altar: The materials we are using today lend themselves to simple design, and the simplicity of Japanese arrangements especially suits them to our needs.

A central arrangement in the Japanese style could be a welcome and exciting change. Tall green or dry bamboo stalks are effective in side arrangements. Try using an azalea branch at the base of these. The soft, fresh bamboo growth of spring combines well with narcissus and daffodils.

49

RACE RELATIONS
Sixth Sunday After Epiphany Day

Symbolism
Love: Red Rose
Humility: Broom
The All-inclusive Love of Christ: Circle

God "hath made of one blood all nations of men" (Acts 17:26) is the
theme for this Sunday. The curved lines in the circle represent the world. The
broom is symbolic of humility and strength. Red roses tell of the love of
God and here are especially meaningful in suggesting the universal
brotherhood of man.

The Altar: A modern, acute hogarth design utilizing a handmade
pottery container of each tones is effective here. Use broom for the
line material and add red roses in a slender line as if they were holding
the world together. Place a single rose on the altar to emphasize the
fact that blood is still shed today in the attempt to achieve brotherhood.

Suggestions: Red gladiolus can be substituted for roses, but they are not quite
as effective and may have to be wired to work into such an
acute hogarth design. You may need to use a water pick
to preserve the freshness of the single rose.

51

REDEMPTION
Seventh Sunday After Epiphany Day

Symbolism
Redemption: Lily

The lily probably has more symbolic meanings than any other flower. It signifies purity, innocence, heavenly bliss, immortal life, and, of course, redemption.

The Altar: A pair of arrangements of lilies and pink gladiolus would be a nice contrast to last week's flowers. If greenery is needed, acuba, ligustrum, camellia, laurel, or lemon foliage would go well with this material. For an altar which calls for a simple arrangement, you might use the foliage with lilies only. Either raised containers of alabaster or white ceramic urns would be suitable holders.

HAPPINESS
Eighth Sunday After Epiphany Day

Symbolism
Happiness: Flowering Spring Branches, Caladium, Tulip
Indestructibility: Acacia

Early spring flowers symbolize happiness, which in Christ is indestructible and everlasting. On this Sunday they may serve also to lift our spirits in a joyous, early expression of springtime.

The Altar: This expression of joy and springtime may be brought out by using forsythia branches and variegated acuba foliage. A free-style design of pink caladium and pussy willow branches can imply a feeling of happiness.
If the arrangement is to be mass, add acacia, a few dutch iris, or yellow tulips.

Suggestions: Let the tulips stand in deep water prior to arranging them. Adding a few pennies to the water in the container often helps these flowers retain their size and condition.

BROTHERHOOD
Ninth Sunday After Epiphany Day

Symbolism

Brotherhood: A Combination of Many Varieties of Flowers

Holy Spirit: Candles

As we observe Brotherhood Sunday, the mass arrangement of different varieties of flowers speaks of our belief in the brotherhood of man while the flames of the candles remind us of our bond with one another through the Holy Spirit.

The Altar: A mass arrangement of colorful spring flowers would be the first choice for this Sunday. However, lemon foliage with white azaleas or a mass arrangement of blue corn flowers and either red or white roses would be good substitutes.

LENT

The Season

The Lenten season begins on Ash Wednesday and continues until Easter; Lent actually lasts for forty days and does not include the six Sundays that fall during that time.* The period commemorates the forty days that Christ fasted and was tempted in the wilderness.

Lent was observed by the church as early as the second century by a brief period of fasting preceding Easter; it was during the seventh century that the period was extended to forty days. Since the observance fell during the early part of the year, it seems to have become confused with the season, and its name is derived from the Anglo-Saxon *lencten,* which means "spring—the time when the days lengthen."

Most Christians consider Lent a time to be devoted to meditation and to strengthening their faith. It is a solemn season of prayer, self-discipline, and penitence in preparation for Easter, the greatest and most joyful of Christian festivals.

The last week of Lent is called Holy Week. It is preceded by Palm Sunday, which marks Jesus' triumphant entry into Jerusalem, when the crowds laid branches of palm trees in the road before him. Maundy Thursday is revered as the day of the Lord's Supper and is followed by Good Friday, the most solemn day of the Christian year, the day of the Crucifixion.

Violet (some churches use purple) is the color used throughout the Lenten season except on Good Friday when the deep black of mourning is traditional. Neither flowers nor candles are appropriate on Good Friday.

*The date of the Annunciation, March 25, will usually fall in Lent. It is celebrated in many churches on the Sunday that comes nearest to the date. It can be found in the special observances section.

PRAYER
First Sunday in Lent

Symbolism
Penitence: Purple Flowers
Devotion: Hosta

Since Lent is a period of penitence in preparation for Easter, the flowers for this first Sunday in the Lenten season have been chosen to express symbolically man's effort toward penitence. The vertical design of subdued shades of violet should suggest hands uplifted in prayer. The prayer theme is also appropriate as this Sunday falls near the observance of the World Day of Prayer.*

The Altar: Twin vertical arrangements of stock and gladiolus might be placed on either side of a single large candle centered on the altar. The stock may be of a deep violet at the base and shade to lighter tones. If tulips are available, they may be substituted for the gladiolus. Hosta foliage finishes the base nicely.

*See special observances section for World Day of Prayer.

PREPARATION
Second Sunday in Lent

Symbolism
The Word: Holy Bible
The Light: Candle
Life: Cyclamen

During Lent as we prepare for Easter, we turn to the Scriptures for guidance. The open Bible represents the Living Word and the candle or candles the presence of the Living Christ. Every Sunday of the year is a commemoration of the first Easter, and the living plant is representative of the message of eternal life.

The Altar: Place the opened Bible in front of a single candle. If this is awkward for your chancel, put the Bible in the center with a candle on either side of it. You may then flank your Bible-candle arrangement with live plants. These should be placed so that their blooms will show to best effect, which may mean that they will have to be tilted slightly, especially if they are hybrid azalea plants.

Suggestions: Be sure the plants are well watered before they are set in place. If it is desirable that only the flowers and foliage show, the pots may be hidden and well secured in whatever placement this necessitates.

RENEWAL
Third Sunday in Lent

Symbolism
The Risen Lord: The Cross
Penitence: Dogwood
Springtime: Lily of the Valley

The name of Lent is taken from the Anglo-Saxon word for spring, so we have taken for our floral theme the renewal of life, the earth's awakening, along with the regeneration of the spirit through penitence. The empty cross indicates spiritual renewal, and the spring flowers symbolize the new life of growing things.

The Altar: An arrangement of spring branches in bloom with small flowers will carry out the theme of renewal quite well. It does not take a great quantity of such flowers to express this simple theme.

If the cross is centered on the Communion table, you may arrange dogwood branches behind it and place a low arrangement of lilies of the valley in front at the base of the cross.

THE ROAD TO CALVARY
Fourth Sunday in Lent

___

Symbolism
Suffering: Thorns
Victory: Rose

Today we use the rose, which represents love, joy, victory, and the Kingdom of God—all of which speak to us of Jesus. The thorns stand for suffering which he endured for us. The beauty of the rose rising from the cruel, ugly thorns can suggest the triumph of the Resurrection, which turned the suffering and sorrow of the Crucifixion into the glorious message of Easter—a suitable theme as we continue our Lenten preparation for that joyous day.

The Altar: A mass arrangement of green thorn branches with deep red roses (Chrysler Imperial) would be pleasing used as a centerpiece on the altar, or a pair of these arrangements would do nicely on either side of the altar. You might combine the hybrid King's Ransom and floribunda Ivory Fashion roses with a few white dutch iris in an alabaster container.

Another alternative would be to make loops of several long branches of a climber rose and anchor the loops securely in a low container. Break the open spaces with a few long-stemmed roses (Sutter's Gold or Eiffel Tower would be good choices).

Suggestion: If the violet paraments of Lent are used in your church, be sure to choose a rose that will make a pleasing contrast with them.

PASSION SUNDAY
Fifth Sunday in Lent

Symbolism
The Five Wounds of Christ: Five Candles
Passion: Holly
Sorrow: Dutch Iris, Cyclamen, Thistle
Penitence: Lavender Statice

The altar has been prepared for this Passion Sunday to express the suffering and sorrow of Jesus. For centuries holly has been symbolic of the passion of Jesus, and the arrangement of the flowers used with the holly speaks of Mary's sorrow for her son.

The Altar: A pair of crescent arrangements placed under and near the cross will give the feeling of supporting the cross. Burfordi holly and thistle make a good combination, or holly may be used with white dutch iris or white cyclamen.

You might try thistle and lavender statice, using two shades of lavender which will represent the color of the season. These are good in a gentle hogarth design. If desired, purple candles may be used with this and placed in whatever manner seems best for your chancel.

PALM SUNDAY
Sixth Sunday in Lent

Symbolism
Victory: Palm
The Gates of the City: Two Candles

Palm Sunday celebrates the triumphant entry of Jesus into Jerusalem.
Two candles are used to represent the gates of the city. The palm leaves
are placed in an upright arrangement between them to express spiritual
victory and the joy of the crowd in welcoming Jesus to Jerusalem.

The Altar: Trim flat, fan-shaped palmetto leaves to a smaller size and arrange
them in a triangular design, using a few white gladiolus for interest.

Suggestions: An all-green plan in an arrangement of sago or royal palm
leaves is a good alternative. Using a Japanese usubata,* design the palm
leaves in a free-style arrangement that expresses the feeling of victory.

*A usubata is a bronze container with a circular top and is used for classical arrangements.

MAUNDY THURSDAY
The First Celebration of the Lord's Supper

Symbolism
Bread: Wheat
Wine: Grapes
Fellowship: Circle

Maundy Thursday commemorates the Last Supper, the time when Jesus celebrated the Feast of the Passover with his disciples and instructed them in the institution of Holy Communion. After dinner he washed the disciples' feet (symbolic of love in service to others), and following this he gave them a new commandment, telling them to love one another as he had loved them. Thus came the name "maundy," which is thought to be derived from the Latin word *mandatum,* meaning "command."

The foot-washing ceremony is now rarely followed on this day, and the significance of Maundy Thursday lies in celebrating the origination of the Communion service. The wheat (bread) and grapes (wine) are arranged in a circular design to express the fellowship of man and his unity with his Lord.

The Altar: Make designs for both sides of the Communion table, using natural bearded wheat and tokay grapes. The wheat and grapes are good in crystal, silver, brass, or soft-toned pottery. Use a chalice-type container. The Communion elements are on the table with the fair linen cloth.

Choose the number of candles appropriate for the type of Communion service being used. Tenebrae service is often held on this night. This calls for a separate candle for each selection of scripture which is read.

Suggestion: Anchor the wheat in dry oasis or styrofoam. Place bunches of fresh grapes at the base by attaching the stems to wooden picks.

GOOD FRIDAY
The Crucifixion

Symbolism
Crown of Thorns
Three Nails
Cross

Nearly every Protestant church observes Good Friday in some way. The church may be open, with black paraments and other symbols of the day in evidence. Many churches hold a three-hour service which emphasizes the full significance of the day. This is a day of mourning—set aside for centuries so that all men shall remember the Crucifixion.

There are no flowers on the altar, only the black paraments. A crown of thorns and three nails are representative of the suffering of our Lord, and the cross forever speaks of that day.

The Altar: Use no flowers in the chancel. A circle of thorns with three nails centered therein may be placed at the foot of the cross. Where it is permissible, the cross may be draped in black crepe. Black paraments are used, but if these are not available, leave the altar, lectern, and pulpit bare.

Suggestion: An arrangement of black thorns and three purple orchids may be used in the narthex if the three-hour service is planned. The orchids would symbolize the three hours on the cross. You may wish to cover the table where these are placed with a black cloth.

EASTERTIDE

The Season

The importance of Easter has been stressed by the long preparation of
Lent culminating in the solemn observances of Holy Week. The joyful
day of Easter now marks the beginning of seven weeks of rejoicing called
Eastertide.

Easter is the oldest, most important, and most joyful festival of the Christian
year. It celebrates Christ's Resurrection on the third day after his Crucifixion.
In its early days the holiday was called the Christian Pasch, the name being
taken from the Hebrew word *pasah,* "to pass over." The origin of the English
name "Easter" is uncertain, although it may be derived from the Anglo-Saxon
goddess of spring, Eostre.

The holiness of Easter cannot be overstated. Not only does its date determine
the date of every movable feast in the church calendar, but the whole year
of worship is built around it. The message of Easter is that of the resurrection
of the body and the life everlasting.

The joy of Eastertide is symbolized by the use of white, the color of rejoicing,
throughout the period.

EASTER DAY
The Risen Lord

Symbolism
The Risen Lord: Lily
Victory: Palm
The Tomb: Stone

Easter, the oldest, most sacred, and most joyful day of the Christian year, calls for special care and reverence in preparing the floral offering.

The lily has come to be the special flower of Easter and is considered symbolic of death and resurrection. As Christ died, was buried, and rose again, so the lily's old plant decays, forms a new bulb in the earth, and sends forth new life again.

There is a tendency to think of using huge masses of lilies at Easter, but often a single lily will express the meaning of the day with greater impact.

The Altar: A good arrangement for a free-standing altar is made by using a large stone shaped like the tomb door. One single lily, symbolizing the risen Lord, lifts its head above the stone. If a calla lily is used, break the point of exit from the stone with a small, trimmed palm leaf following the line of the lily stem. To complete the effect group three potted madonna lilies with a seven-branched candelabrum behind the chancel screen near both the pulpit and the lectern.

As an alternate arrangement duplicate designs of calla or madonna lilies may be placed on opposite sides of the altar (a circular design would be appropriate). A few palm leaves would add the symbol of victory.

Another suggestion for Easter Day would incorporate the crown of thorns, which may have been used on Good Friday. Place this crown directly on the altar table and put a low, round container filled with tall, stately madonna lilies in its center. A few choice stems will be adequate to express the transition from the agony of the cross to the joy of the triumphant resurrection morning. Use only enough foliage to conceal the container.

Suggestion: In the first arrangement protect the table with a folded towel and cover the exposed edges of this cloth with small pebbles.

FOR GOD SO LOVED THE WORLD

First Sunday After Easter Day

Symbolism
Divine Love: Red Rose
Human and Divine Natures of Christ: Two Candles

We have chosen this theme for the first Sunday after Easter Day to acknowledge the measure of God's love for man. The red rose, standing for divine love, may be used in conjunction with the two candles representing the dual nature of Christ to express our remembrance of God's precious gift to man.

The Altar: Between the two candles place a simple triangular arrangement of red roses, adding some green foliage such as eucalyptus or maiden hair or asparagus fern.

Suggestion: For a pleasing effect pink gladiolus might be added to the red roses.

THE NEW LIFE IN CHRIST

Second Sunday After Easter Day

Symbolism
The Old Life: Dead Wood
The New Life: Spring Branches

The risen Christ said, "I am the life," and this statement serves as the theme for today's plan. We emphasize the acceptance of Christ, which prompts one to put off the old self and try to begin again. Thus in our arrangement featuring a weathered stump (or driftwood) with pussy willow branches reaching upward toward the light, we see man reaching for the new life.

The Altar: A weathered stump centered on the altar makes an excellent base for artistically arranged spring branches. Place the branches in a sweeping curve from the base. A few colorful flowers may be placed at the base, but this is not necessary.

Should you require twin arrangements, try some gray driftwood pieces and use crab apple branches for a light spring arrangement. In either arrangement try to give the feeling of life springing from the earth.

THE CHRISTIAN FAMILY
Third Sunday After Easter Day

Symbolism
Life: Green Foliage
Triumph of Divine Love: Morning Glory

This Sunday we stress the importance of a sound family relationship. Love of God can be expressed through our love for one another, and we attempt to extend our love for the members of our own families until it becomes love for the family of man.

Our floral arrangement seeks to express these aims through the use of green foliage for life and morning glories for the divine love which is our goal. The selection of simple garden flowers also carries out the theme of home and family.

The Altar: Rhododendron foliage combined with morning glories in a mass arrangement provides a good interpretation of today's theme. Try hogarth or crescent designs of green spring branches combined with white narcissus. A black container raised on short legs is good.

Suggestion: Alternates could be all-green foliage designs or a combination of spring flowers such as blue iris, lavender tulips, and lilacs with crab apple branches.

FISHERS OF MEN
Fourth Sunday After Easter Day

Symbolism
Hope of Salvation to the Faithful: Bulrush (Cattail)
Devotion: Bamboo
Greatness: Reed
Truth: Lotus

As Jesus walked along the shore of the Lake of Galilee, he called to the fishermen Simon and Andrew, "Come and follow me, and I will teach you to catch men!" It is interesting that the plant life which is found on lakeshore and water's edge can be used to express symbolically Jesus' message, its truth and promise; it is in that message that the secret of "catching men" is found.

The Altar: Make a naturalistic arrangement using cattails with adequate foliage and bamboo at the base. You might make twin arrangements of these materials and place them on either side of the altar table.

As an alternate, use two arrangements of bamboo with lotus foliage at the base of each design.

Reed or the beautiful papyrus plant may be used in either suggested arrangement.

Suggestion: The above materials lend themselves nicely to a moribana arrangement. ("Moribana" means "piled up" flowers in a low bowl. It depicts nature but allows greater freedom in arranging than did previous forms of arrangement.)

THE MINISTRY
*Fifth Sunday After Easter Day**

Symbolism

God's Promise: Willow Branch

Faith: Hyacinth

Endurance: Stock

Courage: Plum Branch

Joy: Daffodil

The emphasis this Sunday is placed on the work of the ministry, and the flowers have been chosen to convey the promise to those of faith: "Go, teach, preach, baptize . . . and I am with you."

The Altar: Tall, graceful arrangements of willow branches accented with white stock or blue hyacinths may be placed on pedestals. This type of arrangement will show up well if there is adequate wall space.

Plum branches and white (Mount Hood) daffodils are lovely in smaller arrangements. A few well-chosen flowers are effective.

*Observed as Aldersgate Sunday in some Methodist churches.

ASCENSION SUNDAY
Sixth Sunday After Easter Day

Symbolism
Truth: Lotus
Friendship: Bamboo, Ivy, Wheat, Rose
Love: Cornflower

After the Resurrection on Easter, Christ spent forty days on earth. On Ascension Day he was taken up to heaven. We are told how he was talking with the disciples when he ascended and was received into a cloud out of their sight.

On this first Sunday after Ascension we will model our flowers on qualities that are unseen but real—love, friendship, truth. These are values which must have helped to bind the disciples together as they faced what they had to do after the ascent of their Lord.

The Altar: Perhaps the most expressive combination for this day would be heavenly blue cornflower and ivy. Lotus combined with bamboo would convey the proper symbolism, as would wheat used with roses. (Either green wheat heads or dried ones are fine; roses should be selected with care.)

A tall, vertical design scaled to your particular setting would be excellent using any of the above combinations.

PENTECOST

The Season

Pentecost covers from eleven to sixteen Sundays; the name is taken from the first Sunday in the season, which falls fifty days after Easter.

Pentecost, one of the three major festivals of the Christian church, is the commemoration of the descent of the Holy Spirit on the disciples after Jesus' Passion, Resurrection, and Ascension. The gift of the Holy Spirit to the disciples occurred as they were celebrating the Jewish Pentecost, or Feast of Weeks.

The Jewish feast began as a thanksgiving for the first fruits of the wheat harvest but later became associated with Moses' receiving the law on Mt. Sinai. The Jewish Pentecost came fifty days after the ceremony of the barley sheaf during Passover. The name is taken from the Greek and means "fiftieth day."

As the Jews had associated Pentecost with the giving of the law and the foundation of their religion, so the Christians felt that the descent of the Spirit superseded the old law and marked the founding of the church.

In northern Europe, Pentecost was a favorite time for baptism, probably due to the fact that the weather was generally warm by then. Thus the festival is also known as Whitsunday, which comes from the popular name White Sunday and refers to the wearing of white by the initiates for the ceremony and for the week following the baptism.

Red, which is symbolic of fire, Christian zeal, and the work and ministry of the church, is used throughout Pentecost in many churches except on Trinity Sunday, when white is used.

PENTECOST (WHITSUNDAY)
The Birth of the Christian Church

Symbolism
Pentecost: Tongues of Flame
Seven Gifts of the Spirit: Seven Candles

On Pentecost, when the Holy Spirit came to the disciples, there appeared
to be cloven tongues of flame resting on each of them. Those flames were the
visible sign of the descent of the Spirit to the apostles, and flame has been
the symbol of that descent ever since.

We will represent the disciples' experience by placing our emphasis on the
tongues of flame.

The Altar: If possible, make one central design to symbolize the seven tongues
of flame. However, if you need twin arrangements, you could use two
torchlike designs. Your arrangement should not be too obvious a reproduction
of the symbol, but should be adequate to convey your idea.

The best choice of flower would be flame-red gladiolus—the color must be
a true fire red. These flowers may be used in a large, low container without
foliage, but with pieces of coal placed at the base of the arrangement for
added meaning. If you wish to use foliage, that of sansevieria or croton
is good; celosia works well at the base.

Flame-colored amaryllis used in vertical designs is expressive and colorful,
or ti leaves can be used exclusively and effectively.

Suggestion: For an additional symbol of flames you may want to try small
vigil candles in red crystal holders.

95

TRINITY SUNDAY
First Sunday After Pentecost

Symbolism
The Trinity: Equilateral Triangle, Three Candles

Acceptance of the Trinity, of the coexistence of Father, Son, and Holy Spirit in the unity of the Godhead, is one of the fundamental tenets of the Christian faith. In view of this it is interesting to note that there were no very early symbols of this doctrine; those we know originated in medieval or modern times and are nearly all geometrical forms used to illustrate the nature of three-in-oneness. This symbolism is frequently found in the architectural design of the church building as well as in the decorative elements.

Today we use the equilateral triangle, a common symbol, designating the equal sides as the three separate persons united in a single element. Three candles which, of course, also represent the Trinity are used on the altar.

The Altar: If you can, use a *single* equilateral triangular design centered on the altar or table. White flowers should be used this Sunday, but you may add just enough foliage or small flowers in color to break the "flat mass" surface. White gladiolus make a good triangular design and can be arranged to avoid the flat-surface effect. Use some of the bud spikes for this purpose.

An alternative might be a combination of blue columbine and white stock with an added touch of baby's breath (gypsophila) to lighten the piece.

GIFTS OF THE SPIRIT: KNOWLEDGE AND WISDOM

Second Sunday After Pentecost*

Pentecost
Second Sunday
Color: Red

Symbolism
Source of Truth: Bible
Seven Gifts of the Spirit: Seven Candles

Today we begin a series of services emphasizing seven gifts of the Holy Spirit. The emphasis this Sunday is on the importance of the Scriptures in our search for *knowledge* and *wisdom,* two gifts of the Spirit.

The Bible represents the source of truth—and truth must be the basis of all knowledge and wisdom. The living plants mean life and growth, and the candles may symbolize both the seven gifts and the light for seeking knowledge.

The Altar: Arrange a row of living caladium plants (green and white) so that the foliage will be shown to best advantage. Use seven tall candles spaced evenly behind the foliage and place the open Bible on the center of the altar.

As an alternative, try a design of lotus blossoms with self foliage. Use this with a seven-branched candelabrum.

*Some churches may observe Student Sunday at this time. See the special observances section for this service.

99

GIFTS OF THE SPIRIT: COUNSEL
Third Sunday After Pentecost

Symbolism
Endurance: Pine
Pure Love: Carnations
Seven Gifts of the Spirit: Seven Candles

Counsel is a third gift of the Spirit and implies the ability to express to others our knowledge of God and his works. We cannot teach others effectively without love, and endurance has always been required to do the work of the church. This is what we are attempting to say by our selection and arrangement of today's materials.

The Altar: Try a design featuring almost vertical twin crescents of pine and carnations placed in front of the symbolic seven candles or on either side of the cross with the lower points facing away from the altar center.

For a central arrangement you could use a triangular design which would give a light, airy effect instead of the usual heavy impression made by pine and carnations.

GIFTS OF THE SPIRIT: UNDERSTANDING
Fourth Sunday After Pentecost

Symbolism
The Trinity: Triangle
Power and Stability: Pine
Seven Gifts of the Spirit: Seven Candles

Understanding, like other gifts of the Spirit, is not easy to achieve or retain. We must work to attain these gifts, and in our attempts we tend to go off on tangents and generally to follow circuitous routes to our goal. This is what we have in mind in our use of the twisted branches. The triangle stands for the Trinity, the source of all understanding, and the pine stands for power and stability.

The Altar: A graceful, free-form triangular design of pine combined with only a few choice flowers and their own foliage would be lovely. To this add some twisted branches or vines to suggest the winding pathways. Placing the flowers in a positive vertical line will emphasize the unvarying direction of our search in contrast to the confused paths we sometimes take.

If you prefer a more conventional arrangement, form a simple, pleasing triangle of peonies with self foliage.

Again, work in your seven candles as you see fit.

GIFTS OF THE SPIRIT: MIGHT

Fifth Sunday After Pentecost

Pentecost
Fifth Sunday
Color: Red

Symbolism
Strength: Iris, Yew
Weakness: Cockleburs
Holy Spirit: Columbine
Seven Gifts of the Spirit: Seven Candles

Today's design is based on the gift of *might*. With the aid of the Spirit we can overcome our weaknesses and attain strength; this we suggest by the use of the strong iris foliage springing from a cluster of cockleburs.

The Altar: An interesting arrangement of long, strong iris foliage with a cluster of wild cockleburs at the base can be used effectively today.

Masses of columbine (choose a color that will go with the parament) with a bit of yew for background green are nice. If the background is not needed, use no foliage. Try a crystal container for the columbine.

Continue to use seven candles or the seven-branched candelabrum in whatever manner seems most appropriate.

GIFTS OF THE SPIRIT: TRUE GODLINESS

Sixth Sunday After Pentecost

Symbolism
Pentecost: Flame
Sword of the Lord: Gladiolus
Love: Rose, Cornflower, Morning Glory
Seven Gifts of the Spirit: Seven Candles

True godliness is the gift of the Spirit we are emphasizing today with a white flame leaping upward from a heart of love. The fire that burns with a white flame is the most potent, and this is what we symbolize as we witness to the Living Christ.

The Altar: Twin vertical designs of white gladiolus and red roses would be suitable on this day. A modern or abstract flame is impressive. Since the white flame is the strongest, use the white gladiolus with a small center of red for the outline of a sweeping, feather-like flame. A center of blue cornflowers or morning glories may stress the presence of love at the heart of the fire.

The seven candles should be used again this Sunday.

Suggestion: Remember that your arrangement should be a good interpretive design and not just a realistic reproduction of the symbol.

GIFTS OF THE SPIRIT: FEAR OF THE LORD
Seventh Sunday After Pentecost

Symbolism
Reverence of Man Before God: Horizontal Design
Adoration: Sunflower
Humility: Violet, Lily of the Valley
Earthly Sorrow and Sin: Thistle
Love: Ivy
Seven Gifts of the Spirit: Seven Candles

A seventh gift of the spirit, *fear of the Lord,* is depicted in the horizontal floral offering which represents man's reverence before God.

The Altar: The horizontal design must be made with special care since it is rarely used on the altar. Be sure to keep the placement of your flowers in mind as you select them. The arrangement can be set directly on the table with the container hidden; however, it may be more effective if it is raised a few inches.

To make your arrangement you might consider the following. Sunflowers, especially the new hybrids, are lovely and need very little foliage. Lilies of the valley with violets and ivy are nice. Lavender thistle, if available at this time, makes a beautiful arrangement.

Suggestion: Use gloves in handling thistle and treat it overnight in deep water before arranging.

Seven candles are still appropriate for use.

BLESSED ARE THE POOR IN SPIRIT

Eighth Sunday After Pentecost

Symbolism
Eternity, Everlasting Life: Circle

Today and for the next seven Sundays we will take the theme for our arrangements from the Beatitudes. This Sunday we are using a circular design to express eternity and everlasting life—the Kingdom that the poor in spirit are promised.

The Altar: Sweet peas in soft hues and baby's breath (gypsophila) are easy to work into a circular design. Other garden flowers available at this season may be used. A mixture of pale roses in shades of pink and yellow is good, or snapdragons or asters with or without baby's breath would be pleasing.

BLESSED ARE THEY THAT MOURN

Ninth Sunday After Pentecost

Symbolism
Sorrow: Marigold, Thistle
Courage: Camomile

The thistle and the marigold are the symbols this Sunday as they represent sorrow, or those who mourn. Using the camomile (a daisy-like aster) with them speaks of the courage with which the Christian faces sorrow, knowing that he has help and comfort close at hand.

The Altar: A mass design of marigolds is simple and provides an opportunity to arrange these flowers as they grow. Marigolds may be used alone in a nice blending of shades of gold and yellow, or the paler yellows by themselves may be more pleasing with the red paraments.

You might add lavender thistle or camomile to the marigolds, or either of these flowers can be used effectively alone. Choose a complementary foliage for the flower you select.

BLESSED ARE THE MEEK
Tenth Sunday After Pentecost

Symbolism
Humility: Violet, Fern

The gentle violet and soft fern are easily recognized as standing for humility; we think of them as growing in obscure spots, perhaps hidden away in the woods. They make an excellent floral interpretation of the meek, of quiet, self-effacing people.

The Altar: Remember that the red paraments are still being used for this season, and be careful to break questionable color combinations with ample foliage. Phlox—or perhaps violets arranged in clusters on stems like phlox—combined with leatherleaf, plumosa, or another strong fern makes a simple, good design.

Lavender phlox may be used on pedestals away from the red paraments, or the exclusive use of ferns is restful on a hot Sunday.

Suggestion: If violets are submerged in water overnight, they will need no water when arranged.

BLESSED ARE THEY WHICH DO HUNGER AND THIRST AFTER RIGHTEOUSNESS

Eleventh Sunday After Pentecost

Pentecost
Eleventh Sunday
Color: Red

Symbolism
Justice: Pear

Fruit is seldom chosen for altar arrangements although it has a long history in traditional Christian symbolism. It can be highly effective; so take the pear, symbol of justice, for today's representation of those who seek righteousness.

The Altar: A design utilizing driftwood could be made to express balance; to this add pears with their own foliage.

It would not be out of place to use a set of scales to balance the fruit of the pear. Your center of worship would, of course, have to be of a type to make this kind of arrangement appropriate.

BLESSED ARE
THE MERCIFUL
Twelfth Sunday After Pentecost

Symbolism
Mercy: Wheat, Willow Branches
Love: Crape Myrtle

Mercy seems indivisible from Christian love; so in our theme based
on the merciful, we combine symbols of mercy—wheat and willow
branches—with one of love—crape myrtle.

The Altar: A vertical design makes a good arrangement, and if two vertical
designs of the chosen materials are placed on either side of the cross, perhaps
on pedestals, they can give the feeling of hands reaching up for mercy. You
might use fresh heads of crape myrtle with an accent of natural bearded
wheat.

Suggestion: It may be desirable to remove all foliage from the myrtle
to give the most effective contrast in materials. If willow branches
are used, the design should be adjusted to utilize the willow to best
advantage; in this case it may be a good idea to remove the myrtle foliage.

119

BLESSED ARE THE PURE IN HEART

Thirteenth Sunday After Pentecost

Pentecost
Thirteenth Sunday
Color: Red

Symbolism
Purity: Orchid, Lily, Gardenia, Orange Blossom

The flowers chosen today to speak of the pure in heart—orchids, orange blossoms, lilies, and gardenias—have traditionally been used as symbols of purity. These delicate flowers are a pleasure to work with, and our task is made easier since they are generally recognized as representing the theme we seek to express.

The Altar: There is considerable leeway in the choice of arrangement for today, but it is essential that the design be kept simple. A spray of cymbidium orchids with wood bark and yew is good. Orange blossoms or gardenias used with their own foliage are lovely; no additional materials are needed. Gardenia plants can be used effectively. One tall stem of regal lilies placed in a crystal or earthenware container expresses the theme nicely. You might wish to try a single white orchid with adequate foliage background.

BLESSED ARE THE PEACEMAKERS

Fourteenth Sunday After Pentecost

Symbolism

Peace: Peace Rose, Mistletoe, Verbena, Olive Branch

The theme of the blessedness of the peacemakers seems especially pertinent at this time, but, in truth, man has always desired peace and never really managed to achieve it.

As our symbol of peace we use the lovely Peace rose, and as our symbol of the confusion and problems that beset our search for peace we use a mass of tangled metal.

The Altar: Choose no more than three long-stemmed roses and arrange them so that they break through the tangled metal to rise above it in a strong statement.

Mistletoe combined with pink crape myrtle in low mass groupings would be an alternate choice.

A single olive branch artistically placed can also give the whole message.

123

BLESSED ARE THEY WHICH ARE PERSECUTED FOR RIGHTEOUSNESS' SAKE

Fifteenth Sunday After Pentecost

Symbolism
Persecution: Thorns

Today we use thorns, a symbol of persecution, to represent the untold numbers of Christians who have suffered for their beliefs. These include missionaries who endure conditions ranging from minor difficulties to severe hardships and who, when necessary, lay down their lives in the service of their Lord.

The Altar: A careful combination of thorns (green from the tree or bush) with miniature zinnias of various shades and colors can express the theme today. Try placing the darker zinnias in the center of the mass design and bringing the flowers in lighter shades farther out.

If you wish to use a pair of arrangements, try thorns with one or two large white chrysanthemums.

125

KINGDOMTIDE

The Season

Kingdomtide includes thirteen or fourteen Sundays; it begins with the Festival of Christ the King on the last Sunday in August and continues until Advent. Labor Day and Thanksgiving are included in the season.

In the traditional church year Pentecost extends from the seventh Sunday after Easter until Advent. Kingdomtide is a new season initiated by the Federal Council of Churches in 1937. Its origin lies in the social gospel movement, and it stresses the principles of the Kingdom of God, the social teachings of Christ, and the responsibilities of all Christians to society.

In those churches which do not observe the season of Kingdomtide, the arrangements that are given here could still be used. The themes used for these floral offerings are of general significance, as all denominations have come more and more to stress social responsibility.

The color for Kingdomtide is green, which signifies life, hope, and growth. White is used on the first Sunday in celebration of the Festival of Christ the King, while red is usually used for Reformation Day and Thanksgiving Day.

FESTIVAL OF CHRIST THE KING

First Sunday in Kingdomtide

Symbolism
Message of Love: Rose
Festival Day: Seven-branched Candelabra

Kingdomtide begins with an emphasis on the preaching ministry of Jesus and with special focus on his message of love and concern for mankind.

As we stress social concerns for the next eight Sundays, we will try to use flowers on the altar which are representative of those growing in the Holy Land.* The wild pink rose, symbolizing love, is to be found climbing over rocks and walls in the hill country while the tall climbing species with white flowers grow in Galilee.

The Altar: Place mass arrangements of wild pink roses in simple containers on pedestals near seven-branched candelabra. The plain thicket rose is ideal for this arrangement if it is available, but a single floribunda in pink or white would be a good substitute. The pips of wild roses in shades of orange-red add the wild flavor to white floribundas.

Flowers of the Holy Land by Bertha S. Vester provides an excellent illustrated resource on Holy Land flowers.

LABOR SUNDAY
Second Sunday in Kingdomtide

Symbolism
Victory: Oleander, Laurel
Gratitude: Dahlia

Labor Sunday provides the opportunity to mark the victories in growth of understanding achieved between labor and management. Oleander and laurel, which we use to represent the victory of improved relations, are natural shrubs of Palestine.

The Altar: Twin arrangements of oleander would be good today. Modern varieties of the flower come in pink, white, salmon, yellow, or crimson. You might substitute laurel or rhododendron. If only the foliage of these plants is available, add dahlias for color.

A CONCERN
FOR THE HEALTH AND
WELFARE OF MAN
Third Sunday in Kingdomtide

Symbolism
Pure Love: Pinks (*Dianthus plumarius*)

The pink symbolically expresses love, which is the basis for charity and our concern for the health and welfare of all mankind. Today we use the small pinks which are native to the United States to represent the Egyptian pink which flourishes in at least three dozen varieties in Palestine.

The Altar: Try a single mass design in a crystal container with only a bit of delicate fern for foliage. Substitute miniature carnations if the pinks are not available. Lavender may be combined with the pinks if additional height is needed.

133

CONCERN OVER JUVENILE DELINQUENCY
Fourth Sunday in Kingdomtide

Kingdomtide
Fourth Sunday
Color: Green

Symbolism
God's Mercy; Earthly Desires: Fig
Forgetfulness: Poppy

The fig plant is probably best known today as standing for man's lust for fulfillment of earthly desires, but since the time of the ancient Hebrews it has also been symbolic of God's mercy and bounty. This double symbolism makes the fig an excellent choice for expressing our concern for youth gone astray and our desire to bring them back to an awareness of the joys of God's Kingdom. The poppy represents the negligence of parents and youth alike who, intent on their own pursuits, forget their responsibilities to each other and to God.

The Altar: Side arrangements of fig foliage with or without fruit may be quite adequate in your situation. If you can obtain a miniature fig plant (*Ficus pumila* or *Ficus radicans*), combine it with poppy blooms in colors complementary to your chancel.

A modern design using a few red poppy blooms with self foliage would be splendid to convey the idea of forgetfulness.

Suggestion: Both the fig and the poppy need special conditioning before they are ready for arranging. Burn the ends of the stems with candle flame or hot water and plunge them into deep, cold water to set for several hours prior to use.

CHRISTIAN EDUCATION SUNDAY

Fifth Sunday in Kingdomtide

Symbolism
Search for Knowledge: Torch
Constancy: Chrysanthemum
Devotion: Cornflower

On Christian Education Sunday our floral arrangement is prepared with man's desire for education, both Christian and secular, in mind. The endless curiosity of man, his constant quest for understanding, and his devotion to learning and to passing his knowledge on are expressed in our use of the torch design.

Our flowers once again are typical of those found in Palestine. Yellow, daisy-like chrysanthemums are common in the Holy Land as are more than twenty species of cornflowers.

The Altar: Yellow chrysanthemums are combined with wheat in an earthenware container. As an alternate, use cornflowers in twin torch designs, combining color shadings for depth.

WORLDWIDE COMMUNION SUNDAY

Sixth Sunday in Kingdomtide

Symbolism
Unity of the Church: Grapevine
The Communion Wine: Grapes
Human and Divine Natures of Jesus: Two Candles

Around the world today Christians take Communion in an expression of their essential unity and equality under God. This service underlines the common ground of all Christ's churches as they join in the observance of the Lord's Supper.

Most rural Palestinian homes have at least a small vineyard nearby, so we continue our use of plants that grow in the Holy Land.

The Altar: The fair white linens will be used today on the table. It may be your custom to continue the green paraments on the pulpit and lectern. Take this opportunity to try the unusual and combine the lovely grapevine with its own fruit for an effective interpretation. Use fresh grapes in a color best suited to your setting. A central, tall hogarth design or a pair of smaller ones in chalice-type containers can be meaningful.

139

LAYMAN'S SUNDAY
Seventh Sunday in Kingdomtide

Symbolism
Victory: Palm
Peace, Hope: Olive and Olive Branch
Hope, Fulfillment of God's Promise: Almond
Jesus, Hope of the World: One Candle

Jesus was very much concerned with the relationship of man to his fellows and regularly admonished people to love one another, to show compassion to humanity, and to endeavor to be one with all mankind. We try to express something of this in our use of palms, olive branches, or almond foliage, with a single candle.

We know, of course, that these plants grow in the Holy Land as they are often mentioned in the Bible.

The Altar: An effective interpretation of this theme is created by using a large white candle (two and a half to three inches in diameter) with a horizontal design of clipped palms. An upturned crescent may be made of almond or olive foliage. A few pinks (dianthus) or small flowers could be added for color.

As an alternative, use the small Russian olive to make two all-green designs of olive foliage.

CONCERN FOR TEMPERATE HOME LIFE

Eighth Sunday in Kingdomtide*

Symbolism
Faithfulness to God: Daisy

The daisy, symbol of faithfulness to God, also stands for cheerfulness, sympathy, and simplicity—all qualities that should be found in the temperate home.

The daisies which grow in Palestine are white, often tinged with pink or purple, so we will choose white daisies for today's arrangement.

The Altar: The large white Marguerite daisy lends itself to line design and free-form style while small white daisies are effective in mass arrangements. Choose the best style for your setting and select a complementary foliage if it is needed.

---

*This Sunday coincides with World Temperance Sunday, which is observed in many churches.

WORLD ORDER SUNDAY
Ninth Sunday in Kingdomtide

Symbolism
The World: Globe
Reliability, Constancy: Chrysanthemum

Our arrangement today represents our goal of a peaceful world where all peoples would live in harmony and understanding. The yellow chrysanthemum (which grows in the Holy Land) symbolizes reliability and constancy— qualities which must become a part of all nations' foreign policies if the goal is ever to be achieved.

The Altar: Do not incorporate the globe in the floral design, but place it nearby as a balancing object. Large mums are available in fall gardens and can be used in tall, vertical arrangements, designs which give the feeling of reaching for a goal. Cylindrical containers are appropriate for this. The chrysanthemum's own foliage is preferred if it is good and strong; however, it may be removed if other foliage is used. Podocarpus or pine add strength if needed.

REFORMATION SUNDAY
Tenth Sunday in Kingdomtide

Symbolism
Access to the Word of God: Open Bible
Faithfulness: Oak Leaves, Maple Leaves

The open Bible is used this Sunday to stand for the freedom of access to the Scriptures, for the right of everyone to read the Word of God for himself, which was one of the results of the Reformation. In the Bible the Christian finds the principles of his faith.

The Altar: Place the Bible on the altar and arrange red candles appropriately. Oak or maple leaves in a fall color harmonious with the paraments can be very effectively arranged today, or red anthurium with ti leaves can give an added symbolism in color.

*Red is the color for Reformation Day (October 31). However, in many churches the Sunday nearest Reformation Day is celebrated as Reformation Sunday and green, the seasonal color, is used.

THE CHURCH
Eleventh Sunday in Kingdomtide

Symbolism
The Church: Ship
Christ's Love: Pear
Unity of the Church: Pomegranate, Grape
Love: Lemon
Wisdom: Peach
Fidelity: Plum
Sin: Apple

We will follow up Reformation Sunday with an attempt to represent the church as it is today. A ship is one of the oldest symbols for the church, so we will use a low, boat-shaped container filled with fruits representing the many virtues and failings, strengths and weaknesses, human and divine elements embodied in the church today.

The Altar: For one central arrangement take a long, low, boat-shaped container of brass or pottery and fill it with the fruits listed above, using the apples sparingly. Grape or pear foliage would be appropriate to tie the arrangement together.

A pair of similar smaller arrangements could be made using lemon instead of pear foliage.

WORLD PEACE SUNDAY
Twelfth Sunday in Kingdomtide

Symbolism
Love: Red
Faith: White
Truth: Blue
Sincere Love: Magnolia Foliage
Strength: Pine

The flowers for World Peace Sunday may be selected in the colors of our nation: red for love, white for faith, and blue for truth. These are valued attributes at any level—personal, national, or international.

The Altar: An urn would be a good container for a mass design of red carnations, white spider mums, and blue-tinted button mums with magnolia foliage. The carnations may also be combined with white stock and blue delphinium and used with pine for strength.

THE GROWTH
OF THE CHURCH
Thirteenth Sunday in Kingdomtide

Symbolism
Growth, Life: Green Plant Foliage

One of the themes of Kingdomtide is that of the growth of the church. This is the basis for the selection of green plant foliage, symbol of life and growth, for the altar arrangement. It also provides an opportunity to use material which, when used with flowers, goes virtually unnoticed.

The Altar: Use green foliage exclusively today, choosing shades and textures which are complementary to each other. "Flowers" may be made of ivy or galax leaves, and these add interest. Hosta, croton, coleus, and eucalyptus are quite good. Don't overlook the possibilities in mahonia and the many varieties of ilex.

All green foliage designs are good in any setting, traditional or contemporary, and can be arranged to suit your needs.

Suggestion: The task of assembling foliage "flowers" is easier if you use 3M glue (available from a florist or office-supply store) instead of florist wire.

NEW LIFE
IN THE CHURCH
Fourteenth Sunday in Kingdomtide

Symbolism
Flaming Spirit: Red Gladiolus
Potential Life: Coals

On the last Sunday in Kingdomtide the altar flowers should express the urgency of the spirit of renewal in the church. The brilliant red flame is symbolic of new life which can and does rise from seemingly lifeless embers.

The Altar: Use a simple design today to express forcibly the theme of renewal. Flowers suggesting dead coals and a burst of brilliant red fire are splendid. Several deep red chrysanthemums at the base of a well-placed flame of gladiolus are ideal.

Darkened, almost dry cockscomb may serve at the base with the same red flame coming from it. Either place your design on a black wooden base or in a low, flat, black container.

SPECIAL DAYS AND SERVICES

There are many special days and services observed by the Christian churches. Not every church celebrates all the special services, and churches may differ in the times they observe the same service. It would be impossible to incorporate floral plans for all special occasions into this book, but those which are more generally observed are included.

Flower arrangements for baptisms, confirmations, weddings and funerals are also to be found in this section, and it is hoped that the floral designer may find ideas and suggestions to help him achieve a suitable arrangement for whatever service his church may hold.

UNIVERSAL BIBLE SUNDAY

Second or Third Sunday in December

Symbolism

The Word and the Spirit: Bible

Endurance: Pine

Reliability: Chrysanthemum

The Sword of the Lord: Gladiolus

The Light of the World: One Candle

The Holy Bible is central to the celebration of this day and is placed at the center of the altar. This symbolizes the important place it occupies in our worship and is a reminder of the importance it should have in our lives. The Word and the Spirit are gifts we wish to remember during the Advent season. The pine for endurance and the chrysanthemum for reliability may suggest these aspects of the Word of God. The single candle stands for the light that Christ, the living Word, brings into the world.

The Altar: Center the altar table with an open Bible elevated so it is easily visible. Near it place a single purple candle. In the same area use a strong vertical arrangement of lavender spider mums and peeled mitsumata branches. The strength of the arrangement emphasizes the influence of the Word.

Suggestions: If you use the Advent wreath, place the Bible in its center. The single lighted candle should be quite near the open Bible regardless of other altar arrangements or altarware. A variation from the Advent wreath would be a central arrangement of pine branches with lavender chrysanthemums. With the traditional Advent wreath, however, the pine and chrysanthemums are quite effective as side arrangements. Red or purple gladiolus could heighten the effect of either of these arrangements.

The colors of the flowers should be chosen with the color of the season in mind, especially if paraments are used. White, of course, is always acceptable.

STUDENT SUNDAY

Symbolism
Knowledge: Torch

The arrangement to honor the students of the church features a torch design symbolizing the torch of knowledge. Learning and education may light the way eventually to wisdom, and this is what we hope for our students.

The Altar: Place a vertical arrangement on either side of the altar. Red or orange gladiolus are ideal for this type of arrangement and might be combined with carnations. Cedar or other evergreens add life to the combination.

Yew with white gladiolus and lotus pods would be an alternate arrangement.

BOY SCOUT SUNDAY
The Sunday Nearest February 8*

Symbolism
Virtue: Magnolia
Loyalty: Pine
Reliability: Chrysanthemum
Devotion: Daffodil
Friendliness: Yellow Rose

Friendliness is a characteristic generally associated with Boy Scouts. We represent this by using yellow roses while magnolia stands for the many virtues the scouting program seeks to instill in its boys.

The Altar: Use a single mass arrangement of deep green magnolia foliage centered with a gentle hogarth of golden yellow roses such as Summer Sunshine. Make the arrangement in a low brass container. Chrysanthemums or daffodils may be substituted for the roses or may be used with short-needle pine. This combination may be best when two arrangements are required.

*February 8, 1910, was the date of the founding of the Boy Scouts of America.

WORLD DAY OF PRAYER

First Friday in Lent

Symbolism
Knowledge: Torch
Generosity: Gladiolus
Devotion: Azalea

World Day of Prayer has its origins in the proposal made in 1887 by the Presbyterian Church in the United States that the churches unite in a national day of prayer. In 1919 the day became the special province of women, and now it is sponsored by the Church Women United of the National Council of Churches.

The day is observed internationally, and the same service is followed in 125 countries. A different theme is used each year.*

The offering on World Day of Prayer is usually given for the advancement of education or the dissemination of educational materials.
Our altar has been planned with this in mind. The torch of knowledge, made of gladiolus for generosity, would seem to carry this idea and yet blend in with whatever theme has been selected for the day.

The Altar: If you have a central freestanding altar, you might prefer a single design of pale lavender gladiolus in the center of the altar. A combination of gladiolus with hosta foliage can be used in making a lovely pair of arrangements.

*Information concerning the theme and the service may be obtained by writing:
Church Women United, National Council of Churches, 475 Riverside Drive, New York, New York 10027.

THE ANNUNCIATION
March 25 *

Symbolism
Mary the Mother of Jesus: Crescent
Purity of the Virgin: Lily

On March 25 we celebrate the Annunciation—the announcement of the Angel Gabriel to the Virgin Mary that she would bear a son called Jesus, who would be the Son of God. The altar flowers have been planned with this in mind.

The crescent represents Mary, the mother of Jesus, while the lily stands for her purity. The combination of these two symbols placed in a supporting position at the base of the cross represents the natural tendency of the mother to share her son's passion.

The Altar: Place a crescent of lilies in a U-shaped design at the foot of the cross. For the foliage large galax leaves, fern, or a slender philodendron foliage will do nicely.

Suggestion: Should the cross be suspended, it may be well to elevate the design by placing it in a raised container.

*Many churches celebrate the Annunciation on the Sunday nearest March 25.

MOTHER'S DAY
Second Sunday in May

Symbolism
Reliability, Constancy: Chrysanthemum
Mary, the Mother of Jesus: Crescent

For the observance of Mother's Day we have chosen the chrysanthemum, which stands for the motherly virtues of reliability and constancy. The chrysanthemums are arranged in a crescent design, symbolic of Mary, the mother of Jesus.

The Altar: In forming the crescent arrangement of chrysanthemums, use several shades of the chosen color, placing the deepest shades in the central focal point. For combination with the chrysanthemums choose pine, which will serve as good line material.

Suggestion: You may substitute red roses for love or white ones for purity. Peonies, carnations, syringa, azaleas, and forget-me-nots are all good for this theme.

FATHER'S DAY
Third Sunday in June

Symbolism
Constancy: Bulrush (Cattail)
Fidelity: Carnation
Love: Ivy
Strength: Iris

We think of the fatherly qualities as being those of strength, love, and constancy or fidelity. These traits are symbolized by our choice of flowers for today, and in our arrangement we especially stress fidelity.

The Altar: Use a central arrangement of carnations with cattails for strong line emphasis. This same combination could easily be utilized in two smaller designs if your altar requires it.

Garden-grown bearded iris with their own foliage would be excellent in a simple design, or carnations (use one of the many interesting colors available at this time of year) are pleasing in combination with ivy.

Suggestion: Remember in planning your flowers that the paraments for this day will be red.

ALL SAINTS' DAY

November 1*

Symbolism
Bereavement, Sorrow: Marigolds
Everlasting Life: Evergreens
Remembrance of the Deceased: Candles

All Saints' Day is dedicated to the members of the church who have died in the past year. The marigolds represent our sorrow over losing them, the evergreens speak of eternal life, and the candles burn both in memory of the dead and as a symbol of God's presence.

The Altar: This should be an opportunity to use the last marigolds of the season. You may use whatever color or color combinations are available with a bit of yew, pine, or any other evergreen. These materials should work well in a hogarth design in a pair of crescents, or in a mass design with the color shadings carefully planned.

In a small church you could use a candle for each member who died in the past year; where this is not practical, use whatever number seems best to you.

*This service is often observed on the Sunday nearest November 1.

THANKSGIVING DAY
Fourth Thursday in November

Symbolism
God's Goodness to Us: Fruits of the Harvest

Thanksgiving, as we all know, originated as the celebration of a starving people at the time of their first harvest. It is a national holiday, celebrated on the fourth Thursday in November. We recall that first giving of thanks for abundant crops as we place fruits of the harvest on the altar today.

The Altar: Fruit and vegetables should be assembled directly on the altar table; they might be arranged around a choice pumpkin. Flowers and foliage, set in water picks for easy handling, should be used for accent only. Corn husks add texture, but use restraint in employing dried material.

If height is needed, use a tall spike of dried mullein placed as if lifted in praise. A shock of wheat with fruits and vegetables can be effective.

BAPTISM

Symbolism
Grace: Fern, Willow
Rite of Baptism: Water

From the beginning of Christianity, baptism has been considered the gateway to the church. For this reason many of the old churches had the font placed near the church entrance, and it is still so placed in some churches today.

Baptism is an important ritual of all Christian churches and marks the acceptance of the duties and responsibilities of Christianity by the adult; or in the case of a child, it marks the adults' promises to see that the child grows up to accept these responsibilities. The church believes that God uses baptism to claim his own and to put his seal upon them in a unique way.

The Altar: Place tall, graceful woodwardia fern fronds in clear crystal vases on either side of the altar and make certain that the water level in the vases can be seen. This is symbolic of baptism as an outward and visible sign of the grace of Christ.

If you wish to use flowers, daisies would be appropriate—especially for the baptism of children or infants.

For a freestanding altar a beautiful clear crystal bowl of water would be a lovely expression of the symbolism. Fern plants might be placed in the chancel.

If a baptistry tank is used, willow branches arranged about it would be quite effective.

CONFIRMATION

Symbolism
The Word: Open Bible
Fellowship of Christ's Holy Church: Circle

Traditionally, children have been brought into Christian churches at an early age through the sacrament of baptism, and it has been felt that when they reached the age of accountability, they should speak for themselves and confirm their acceptance of Christian responsibilities. Thus confirmation was begun in the ancient church and is continued today. Confirmation marks the full acceptance by the older child or the adult of the Christian faith as contained in the Scriptures as well as his entry into the fellowship of the church.

The Altar: Place the Holy Bible in the center of the altar; it should be opened and raised so that it may be easily recognized. Circular mass arrangements of seasonal flowers are appropriate to use with it. Hyacinths in the spring and dahlias with goldenrod in the fall are good choices. Pine branches with cones are good any time.

MARRIAGE

Symbolism
Love: Rose, Peony, Carnation
Faithfulness: Forget-me-not
Humility: Broom

The wedding held in the church is a religious service, a fact which should be kept in mind at all times while planning the decorations. Many churches have stringent rules on where flowers may be placed for a wedding, so it is a good policy to work closely with the minister or a representative of the church when considering the floral arrangements. By exercising restraint in decoration a solemn beauty can be achieved which underscores the dignity and joy of the ceremony.

White flowers are usually chosen for wedding decoration; however, it may be desirable to use a touch of color as well to harmonize with the bridesmaids' dresses and/or flowers.

The Altar: In a contemporary setting where a central design is needed, you might utilize two arrangements, one slightly higher than the other, and join the two with loops representing the wedding rings. A single white rose should be placed in the center of each loop. The loops can be made of metal painted gold or white.

FUNERAL

Symbolism
Eternity: Canna, Stock
Resurrection and Life: Evergreens, Lily
Love: Rose, Carnation

The Christian funeral should be a joyful service of worship, not a mournful surrender to death. It presents an opportunity for us to express praise and thanksgiving to God for the gifts of life and of eternal life, and it is these gifts that we shall symbolize in our floral offering.

Flowers for a funeral should be arranged and placed in the chancel where they are normally used, although some flowers might be used at the church entrance. The flowers sent by friends are more appropriate for display at the home or the cemetery.

The Altar: Combine red cannas with white stock, utilizing the canna foliage for background material (maroon shades are the best choice in the foliage).

An asymmetrical design of pine or blue spruce with madonna lilies would be an interesting and lovely interpretation of eternal life. Or twin mass arrangements of evergreens with a few lilies may be placed on either side of the altar. In either of these designs the lilies should be used sparingly to express their symbolic meaning clearly. Roses or carnations may be substituted when lilies are not available.

SYMBOLISM IN FLOWERS

Themes and Ideas and Symbolic Materials to Express Them

ABNEGATION: Christmas rose (Helleborus niger)
ABUNDANCE: bamboo, gladiolus, olive branch
ACCEPTABILITY: almond
ACCOMPLISHMENT: laurel
ADORATION: sunflower
ANIMOSITY: aconite (monkshood)
ANXIETY: reed
ARROGANCE: snapdragon
AUTHORITY: crocus
AVARICE: lupine

BEAUTY: delphinium, fern, gladiolus
BENEVOLENCE: daffodil, narcissus, poplar branch, tulip
BEREAVEMENT: marigold
BONDAGE: bitter herbs
BOUNTIFULNESS: wheat
BURNING BUSH: bramble

CHARITY: plane tree (buttonwood or sycamore), tulip, water lily
CHASTITY: camellia, gardenia, lotus, orange blossom
CHEERFULNESS: daisy
CHRIST'S LOVE: pear
COMMUNION:
fruit of the vine—grapes
bread of life—wheat, corn ears, grain
CONCEIT: hydrangea
CONGENIALITY: peach
CONSOLATION: poppy
CONSTANCY: bamboo, bulrush, cedar, chrysanthemum, flowering almond, hyacinth, ivy, plum branch, sunflower, violet
CONTENTMENT: camellia, pine branches
CONTINUITY: dogwood
COURAGE: camomile, plum branches

CROSS: aspen, dogwood
CROWN: chestnut burrs, holly, thorns
CRUCIFIXION: anemone, thorns

DANGER: pitcher plant (Nepenthes)
DEATH: cyclamen (sorrow), cypress
DECISION: foxglove
DELIGHT: caladium
DEVOTION: azalea, bamboo, cornflower, daffodil, hawthorn, hosta, narcissus, rhododendron
DIGNITY: chrysanthemum, peony, regal lily, thistle
DISBELIEF: tritoma (flame-flower)
DISTRUST: apricot
DIVINE APPROVAL: almond
DOMESTICITY: camellia
DOUBT: apricot
DUTY: plum branch

ELEGANCE: lily, white crocus
ENCOURAGEMENT: goldenrod
ENDURANCE: bamboo, oak, pine
ETERNITY: canna, ivy, laurel, oak, stock
EUCHARIST: see Communion

FAITH, FAITHFULNESS: carnation, daisy, forget-me-not, hyacinth, ivy, maple leaves, oak leaves, pine
FERTILITY: fig, pomegranate, poppy
FIDELITY: bamboo, bleeding heart, carnation, ivy, lemon, plum, syringa (mock orange)
FIRST LOVE: lilac
FORCE: oak
FORGETFULNESS: poppy
FORGIVENESS: oak
FRANKNESS: fern
FRIENDSHIP: acacia, bamboo, ivy, lilac, pansy, rose, wheat stems, willow branches

GENEROSITY: gladiolus, orange tree
GLORY: hibiscus, laurel
GOD'S GOODNESS: olive branch
GOD'S LOVE: vine
GOD'S PROMISE: willow branch
GOOD WILL: holly
GRACE: fern, willow branch
GRATITUDE: dahlia
GREATNESS: reed
GRIEF: marigold, thorn

HAPPINESS: bamboo, jasmine, lily of the valley, orange blossom, tulip
HARDIHOOD: clematis
HAUGHTINESS: snapdragon
HEALTH: iris
HEARTACHE: calendula
HOLY SPIRIT: columbine
HONOR: laurel
HOPE: arbutus, flowering almond, forget-me-not, gentian, olive branch, pomegranate, primrose
HOSTILITY: aconite (monkshood)
HUMILITY: broom, fern, lily of the valley, violet

IDEALISM: petunia
IMMORTALITY: acacia, cypress, ivy, lily, lotus, yew
IMPATIENCE: balsam, touch-me-not
INCARNATION: gladiolus
INDECISION: thoroughwort
INDEPENDENCE: thistle
INDESTRUCTIBILITY: acacia
INNOCENCE: daisy, freesia, lily
INTEGRITY: pine

JEALOUSY: calendula
JOY: caladium, chrysanthemum, daffodil, holly, iris, narcissus, poinsettia, rose
JUSTICE: apple, gentian, pear blossoms

KINDNESS: tulip
KINGDOM OF GOD: rose

LIFE: bamboo, evergreens, fig, myrtle, pine, plum branches
LONELINESS: bulrush
LOVE: anemone, azalea, bachelor's button, calendula, carnation, cornflower, forget-me-not, hollyhock, ivy, lemon, lotus, magnolia, morning glory, myrtle, narcissus, pansy, pear, peony, pinks (Dianthus plumarius), rhododendron, rose, syringa, tuberose

LOVELINESS: magnolia, white jasmine
LOYALTY: pine

MAJESTY: lotus, regal lily, strelitzia
MARRIAGE: ivy
MARTYRDOM: rose, strawberry
MARY: almond, cedar (healing qualities), cyclamen (her sorrows), iris, jasmine (fragrance), madonna lily, pear, rose
MEMORY: ivy, smilax, sweet pea, sweet william
MERCY: fig, wheat stem, willow branch
MESSENGER: Siberian iris
MESSIANIC PROMISE: poinsettia, rose
MODERATION: azalea
MODESTY: chrysanthemum, lily, violet
MOURNING: cypress
MUSIC: reed

NATIVITY: Christmas rose (Helleborus niger), Glastonbury thorn
NOBILITY: orchid

PARADISE: palm branches
PASSION OF CHRIST: dandelion, holly, poppy
PATIENCE: onion flowers
PEACE: hollyhock, hyacinth, mistletoe, myrtle, olive branch, verbena
PENITENCE: dogwood, violet
PERFECTION: lotus
PERSECUTION: thorns
PLIANCY: bamboo
POWER: hyacinth, peony, pine
PRAISE: arbutus
PRAYER: blueberry
PRIDE: amaryllis
PROSPERITY: fir, narcissus, oak, pine
PROTECTION: holly
PROTECTIVENESS: elm
PURE HEART: baby's breath, white hollyhock
PURITY: camellia, cherry blossoms, gardenia, hyssop, iris, lily, lily of the valley, lotus, orange blossom, orchid, pear blossom, violet, white cosmos white rose

REDEMPTION: lily
REJOICING: rose
RELIABILITY: chrysanthemum
REMEMBRANCE: pansy, rosemary branches, zinnia
RESPECT: sunflower
RESTFULNESS: sedum

RESURRECTION: gourd, lily, lotus, pomegranate, sheaf of wheat
REWARD: laurel
RIGHTEOUSNESS: apple, gentian, strawberry
RUGGEDNESS: clematis

SADNESS: calendula, gerbera
SALVATION: apple, bulrush (cattail)
SELFLESSNESS: Christmas rose (Helleborus niger)
SELF-LOVE: narcissus
SERENITY: willow branch
SILENCE: peace
SIMPLICITY: daisy, hollyhock
SIN: apple, thistle
SINCERITY: anemone, fern
SORROW: cyclamen, iris, marigold, thistle
SPIRITUALITY: lotus
SPLENDOR: Euonymus japonica
SPRINGTIME: crocus, lily of the valley
STABILITY: peony
STEADFASTNESS: bamboo
STRENGTH: bamboo, broom, cedar, elm, iris, oak, pine, willow branches, yew
SUBMISSIVENESS: forsythia
SUFFERING: rose thorns
SWEETNESS: delphinium
SWORD OF THE LORD: gladiolus
SYMPATHY: bleeding heart, daisy

TEMPERANCE: azalea
TEMPTATION: eucalyptus, lycoris
TENACITY: broom branches
THANKSGIVING: sheaf of wheat
TORTURE: thorns
TRINITY: anemone, clover, shamrock, strawberry foliage, white iris
TRIUMPH: laurel
TRUTH: anemone, bittersweet, lotus

UNITY: grapevine, Job's tears, pomegranate
UPRIGHTNESS: bamboo

VENGEANCE: thistle
VICTORY: laurel, nasturtium, oleander, palm, rose, spirea
VIGOR: plum branches
VIRTUE: cedar branches, cherry branches, magnolia
VITALITY: iris, plum branches

WEAKNESS: cockleburs
WEALTH: peony
WELCOME: wisteria
WELL-BEING: delphinium
WISDOM: dandelion, lotus, peach
WORKS: cherry

YOUTH: daisy

A TABLE OF THE DAYS
ON WHICH EASTER DAY
AND OTHER DAYS DEPENDENT UPON IT
WILL FALL

A.D. 1968-2000

Year	Sundays After Epiphany	Ash Wednesday	Easter Day	Ascension Day	Pentecost	Sundays After Pentecost	Sundays in Kingdomtide*	First Sunday in Advent
1968	8	Feb 28	Apr 14	May 23	June 2	11	14	Dec 1
1969	6	Feb 19	Apr 6	May 15	May 25	13	13	Nov 30
1970	5	Feb 11	Mar 29	May 7	May 17	14	13	Nov 29
1971	7	Feb 24	Apr 11	May 20	May 30	12	13	Nov 28
1972	6	Feb 16	Apr 2	May 11	May 21	13	14	Dec 3
1973	9	Mar 7	Apr 22	May 31	June 10	10	14	Dec 2
1974	7	Feb 27	Apr 14	May 23	June 2	11	14	Dec 1
1975	5	Feb 12	Mar 30	May 8	May 18	14	13	Nov 30
1976	8	Mar 3	Apr 18	May 27	June 6	11	13	Nov 28
1977	7	Feb 23	Apr 10	May 19	May 29	12	13	Nov 27
1978	5	Feb 8	Mar 26	May 4	May 14	14	14	Dec 3
1979	8	Feb 28	Apr 15	May 24	June 3	11	14	Dec 2
1980	6	Feb 20	Apr 6	May 15	May 25	13	13	Nov 30
1981	8	Mar 4	Apr 19	May 28	June 7	11	13	Nov 29
1982	7	Feb 24	Apr 11	May 20	May 30	12	13	Nov 28
1983	6	Feb 16	Apr 3	May 12	May 22	13	13	Nov 27
1984	9	Mar 7	Apr 22	May 31	June 10	10	14	Dec 2
1985	6	Feb 20	Apr 7	May 16	May 26	12	14	Dec 1
1986	5	Feb 12	Mar 30	May 8	May 18	14	13	Nov 30
1987	8	Mar 4	Apr 19	May 28	June 7	11	13	Nov 29
1988	6	Feb 17	Apr 3	May 12	May 22	13	13	Nov 27
1989	5	Feb 8	Mar 26	May 4	May 14	14	14	Dec 3
1990	8	Feb 28	Apr 15	May 24	June 3	11	14	Dec 2
1991	5	Feb 13	Mar 31	May 9	May 19	13	14	Dec 1
1992	8	Mar 4	Apr 19	May 28	June 7	11	13	Nov 29
1993	7	Feb 24	Apr 11	May 20	May 30	12	13	Nov 28
1994	6	Feb 16	Apr 3	May 12	May 22	13	13	Nov 27
1995	5	Mar 1	Apr 16	May 25	June 4	11	14	Dec 3
1996	6	Feb 21	Apr 7	May 16	May 26	12	14	Dec 1
1997	5	Feb 12	Mar 30	May 8	May 18	14	13	Nov 30
1998	7	Feb 25	Apr 12	May 21	May 31	12	13	Nov 29
1999	6	Feb 17	Apr 4	May 13	May 23	13	13	Nov 28
2000	9	Mar 8	Apr 23	June 1	June 11	10	14	Dec 3

*Kingdomtide always begins with the last Sunday of August.

THE CARE OF EQUIPMENT

Not every church is equipped with a sacristy or special storage room, but it is essential to set aside some area in which to care properly for the chancel furnishings and altarware of the church. A place that is easily accessible to the chancel should be provided and ideally should include a sink with a work counter, hot and cold water, and refrigeration, as well as ample storage space. This is the place to keep mechanics for flower arranging, cleaning materials, and tools. Supplies and equipment properly stored and maintained will last longer and require less strenuous cleaning. And, of course, a convenient area and proper supplies facilitate flower arrangement and Communion preparations.

FURNITURE AND FURNISHINGS. Soap and water and a good coat of wax are sufficient treatment for wooden furniture, and dusting weekly, with a thorough cleaning periodically, keeps wood in good condition. Stone, pieces of marble, and granite require little care other than dusting. Stone manufacturers will supply safe instructions for refinishing or sand cleaning. Be sure that a very reliable contractor handles this special work.

The altar or Communion table will probably be your most valuable and beautiful piece of furniture. Today we find that it may be made of stone, wood, metal, or glass —a wide choice of materials, each requiring special care. The altar table can be protected by a cover of glass or plexiglass to provide minimum maintenance and protection from water and tallow damage.

The baptismal font usually is of the same material as the altar table and will require similar care. Fresh water should be provided for each service, emptied after use, and the font thoroughly cleaned. A plastic insert in the font or bowl will reduce maintenance. The same cleaning and filling of the bapistry is also needed.

The paraments, which include the linens and hangings, need good storage for protection and long life. Regular cleaning by a reliable dry cleaner should be adequate for the hangings. Try to store them so that pressing is not required when they are removed for use. The fair linen may be washed by hand; this service is usually the responsibility of the Communion stewards.

Flags require little care since the manufacturer usually provides a cover. It is permissible to mend, dry-clean, or wash a flag. Between services it should be furled (wrapped around the staff) and then cased (wrapped with a cover).

CANDLES. The beeswax content determines the life and effective flame of candles. It is wise, if you have adequate storage space and temperature control, to purchase candles in quantity from a reliable manufacturer. Fresh candles for each service are desirable but not necessary as long as the proper relationship to the altarware is maintained.

Candles may be cleaned by wiping them with a cloth dipped in turpentine. Use warm water to remove all drippings from candles and candleholders before each service. Using waxsavers will reduce this care and will prolong the life of the candles; metal ones are preferable and may be bought to match your holders. To remove the waxsavers, simply hold them under hot water briefly.

To remove wax from linen or silk, lift it gently from the cloth with a sharp knife. If stain or wax remains, press with a hot iron over a blotter. This same procedure is recommended for removing wax from a carpet. When dripless candles are not used, it may be wise to protect your carpet and furniture with a clear plastic cloth beneath the candleholder.

ALTARWARE AND OTHER APPOINTMENTS. Prior to cleaning any church appointment determine its finish and follow the instructions which most manufacturers include with their product. Many items have a protective coating of lacquer; especially lasting are the baked coatings and the silicone types. A weekly dusting or wiping with a soft flannel cloth will clean gold and silver items with a protective coating and will not hurt a lacquer finish. Dampen a soft cloth to remove perspiration stains and then dry with another clean cloth. It is wise to wear soft cotton gloves when handling appointments.

Do not use polish, chemically treated polishing cloths, or harsh detergents on coated appointments as these products will mar the finish and necessitate recoating the articles. Tarnishable items which are not frequently used are best kept in a closed bag or roll of impregnated cloth made especially for this purpose. This will prevent tarnish indefinitely. Store your appointments in a clean, dry area and place them so that no edges or corners can rub on each other.

Wax spots on appointments can best be removed by rubbing them gently with warm cloths. Warm water will loosen wax, but be sure the appointment is dried thoroughly afterward.

In order to prolong the life of metal vase liners, remove these from the vases frequently, wash, and dry well. This will prevent their becoming stuck in the vases. Fiber glass liners do not stick or fuse into metal vases. It is best to have vases with liners that have either rings or good lips for easy removal.

ALUMINUM AND CHROME PLATE. These metals may be cleaned with warm water and soap. Follow this with a good metal polish if necessary.

BRASS AND GOLD. These materials when constantly handled require only routine dusting and occasional washing to maintain their gleaming radiance. Use a mild soap and warm water, rinse, and dry thoroughly with a soft, clean cloth. Fingerprints often found on offering plates may be removed with a damp cloth; the plates should be wiped dry.

STERLING AND SILVER PLATE. The same attention is required that you would give silverware in your home. The new silver polishes with tarnish-preventive formulas eliminate the constant chore of polishing. One application of this on silver plate or sterling not only cleans and polishes, but creates an invisible shield that seals out tarnish for months. Purchase a dusting cloth made by a reputable manufacturer, making sure it is not abrasive, and follow instructions on the container carefully. Polish silver plate no more than is necessary because each rubbing removes some silver.

REFINISHING AND REPLATING. Ultimately, refinishing and replating may be necessary to return your appointment to its original beauty. Today's methods require specialized equipment and techniques.

One takes a chance in doing a home job or employing a finisher who is accustomed to doing commercial work. Seek the services of a manufacturer of church appointments or someone familiar with doing quality church refinishing and replating. The manufacturer will be responsible for the appointment and will be in a position to replace easily any parts or pieces which could become lost or damaged.

BIBLIOGRAPHY

ARCHITECTURE

Biéler, André. *Architecture in Worship*. Philadelphia: The Westminster Press, 1965.

Christ-Janer, Albert, and Foley, Mary Mix. *Modern Church Architecture*. New York: McGraw-Hill Book Company, 1962.

Hunt, Fern Bowers. *Floral Decorations for Your Church*. Philadelphia: Chilton Book Company, 1960.

Stafford, Thomas A. *Within the Chancel*. Nashville: Abingdon Press, 1955.

White, James F. *Protestant Worship and Church Architecture*. New York: Oxford University Press, 1964.

SYMBOLISM—THE CHRISTIAN YEAR

Dunkle, William F., Jr. *Values in the Church Year*. Nashville: Abingdon Press, 1959.

Freehof, Lillian S., and Bandman, Lottie C. *Flowers and Festivals of the Jewish Year*. New York: Hearthside Press, 1964.

Gibson, George M. *The Story of the Christian Year*. Apex ed.; Nashville: Abingdon Press, 1945.

Ickis, Marguerite. *The Book of Religious Holidays and Celebrations*. New York: Dodd, Mead & Co., 1966.

Mullins, Ruth E. *Flowers and Symbols of the Christian Year*. New York: Hearthside Press, 1967.

Wetzler, Robert P., and Huntington, Helen. *Seasons and Symbols*. Minneapolis: Augsburg Publishing House, 1962.

SYMBOLISM—GENERAL

Burke, A. C., ed. *The Language of Flowers*. Los Angeles: Price/Stern/Sloan Publishers, 1965.

Cross, F. L., ed. *Oxford Dictionary of the Christian Church*. New York: Oxford University Press, 1957.

Daves, Michael. *Meditations on Early Christian Symbols*. Nashville: Abingdon Press, 1964.

Ferry, Ervin S. *Symbolism in Flower Arrangement*. New York: The Macmillan Company, 1958.

Gouker, Loice. *A Dictionary of Church Terms and Symbols*. Norwalk, Conn.: The C. R. Gibson Co., 1964.

Lehner, Ernst. *The Picture Book of Symbols*. New York: Tudor Publishing Co., 1956.

McGee, Ratha Doyle. *Symbols, Signposts of Devotion*. Rev. ed.; Nashville: The Upper Room, 1962.

Post, W. Ellwood. *Saints, Signs and Symbols*. New York: Morehouse-Barlow Co., 1962.

Rest, Friedrich. *Our Christian Symbols*. Philadelphia: United Church Press, 1954.

Stafford, Thomas A. *Christian Symbolism in the Evangelical Churches*. Apex ed.; Nashville: Abingdon Press, 1942.

FLOWER ARRANGING

Arnett, Dessie Ash, and Clark, Lenace R. *Methodist Altars*. New ed.; Charleston, W. Va.: Privately printed, 1961.

Benz, M. *Flowers: Free Form, Interpretive Design*. Houston: San Jacinto Publishing Co., 1960.

Bode, Frances. *Creativity in Flower Arrangement*. New York: Hearthside Press, 1967.

191

Clements, Julia. *The Julia Clements Colour Book of Flower Arrangements*. Princeton, N. J.: D. Van Nostrand Co., 1965.

Kroh, Patricia. *Design with Flowers, Unlimited*. Garden City: Doubleday & Co., 1959.

McClinton, Katharine M. *Flower Arrangement in the Church*. New York: Morehouse-Barlow Co., 1944.

Moffitt, Oleta Staley. *Arranging Flowers for the Church*. Philadelphia: Fortress Press, 1959.

Mullins, Ruth E. *Religious Themes in Flower Arrangement*. New York: Hearthside Press, 1959.

Patterson-Knight, Francis, and Saint Claire, Margaret McReynolds. *Arranging Flowers for the Sanctuary*. New York: Harper & Row, 1961.

Rockwell, F. F., and Grayson, Esther C. *Rockwell's New Complete Book of Flower Arrangement*. Garden City: Doubleday & Co. 1960.

Sato, Shozo. *The Art of Arranging Flowers: Japanese Ikebana*. New York: Harry N. Abrams, 1966.

Wilson, Adelaide B. *Flower Arrangement for Churches*. New York: M. Barrows & Co., 1952.

———— and Wilson, Lois. *Flowers for Your Church*. New York: M. Barrows & Co., 1967.

GENERAL

Buttrick, George, ed. *The Interpreter's Dictionary of the Bible*. 4 vols. Nashville: Abingdon Press, 1962.

Goldsmith, Margaret O. *A Bible Garden*. Nashville: Abingdon Press, 1960.

Vester, Bertha Spafford. *Flowers of the Holy Land*. Garden City: Doubleday & Co., 1962.

Photographs: Richard T. Lee
Designer: Nancy Bozeman
Type: Optima
     10 pt., leaded 3 pts.
Typesetter: Parthenon Press
Manufacturer: Parthenon Press
Printing Process: Offset—4-color process
Paper: Body—70# Warren's Patina
     Endsheets—80# Andorra Text, Felt finish laid—Cinnamon
Binding: 2-piece Holliston Payko 1575 Black
     and 80# Andorra Text, Felt finish laid—Cinnamon

DATE DUE

JUN 27		
SEP 11 '69		
DEC 9 '69		
DEC 11 '75		
DEC 6 '71		
DEC 2 '75		
E		
MAY 3 '83		
MAY 2 1983		
GAYLORD		PRINTED IN U.S.A.